# Tackling Tomorrow Today

Courtesy of The Venus Project
Designed by Jacque Fresco and Roxanne Meadows

**Tackling Tomorrow Today**

Volume Two
# America:
# Moving Ahead

Edited by Arthur B. Shostak, Ph.D.

Emeritus Professor of Sociology,
Department of Culture and Communication
Drexel University, Philadelphia, PA 19104

CHELSEA HOUSE
PUBLISHERS
A Haights Cross Communications Company

Philadelphia

303.49
Tac

**CHELSEA HOUSE PUBLISHERS**

VP, NEW PRODUCT DEVELOPMENT  Sally Cheney
DIRECTOR OF PRODUCTION  Kim Shinners
CREATIVE MANAGER  Takeshi Takahashi
MANUFACTURING MANAGER  Diann Grasse

**Staff for TACKLING TOMORROW TODAY**

EXECUTIVE EDITOR  Lee Marcott
EDITOR  Christian Green
PRODUCTION EDITOR  Noelle Nardone
PHOTO EDITOR  Sarah Bloom
SERIES AND COVER DESIGNER  Takeshi Takahashi
LAYOUT  EJB Publishing Services

A Haights Cross Communications◄ Company

http://www.chelseahouse.com

First Printing

9 8 7 6 5 4 3 2 1

Library of Congress Cataloging-in-Publication Data

Tackling tomorrow today / edited by Arthur B. Shostak.
    p. cm.
  Includes bibliographical references and index.
  ISBN 0-7910-8401-9 (v. 1) -- ISBN 0-7910-8402-7 (v. 2) -- ISBN 0-
7910-8403-5 (v. 3) -- ISBN 0-7910-8404-3 (v. 4)  1. Twenty-first
century--Forecasts. 2. Technology and civilization. I. Shostak,
Arthur B.
  CB161.T33 2004
  303.49'09'05--dc22
                                        2004016198

All links and web addresses were checked and verified to be correct at the time
of publication. Because of the dynamic nature of the web, some addresses and
links may have changed since publication and may no longer be valid.

■

*Dedicated to forecasters,*
*prominent and unsung alike,*
*who help us see further,*
*imagine more,*
*prepare better*
*and*
*savor life's extraordinary possibilities.*

■

*There is nothing permanent except change.*
—Heraclitus

■

*To keep our faces toward change*
*and behave like free spirits*
*in the presence of fate*
*is strength undefeatable.*
—Helen Keller

## ACKNOWLEDGMENTS

Sixteen high school students from six states and the District of Columbia volunteered to critique well over sixty candidate essays and help me choose fifty-eight for the four volumes in this series. Their cogent and insightful feedback (266 brief reviews) can be found at the rear of each volume, and it makes clear my considerable debt to them: Amelia Adams, Mike Antonelli, Erin Bauerle, Patricia Marie Borrell, Andrew Crandall, Alex Dale, Tom Dunn, Rebecca Henderson, Mara James, Sarah Konner, Ginger Lemon, Kelly Ramirez, Dalea Reichgott, Benjamin Samuels, Brittany Tracy, and Jessica Varzaly. Special thanks go to Alex, Dalea, Mike, and others for survey responses, and for sheer output alone, to Tom, Jessica, Benjamin, Mara, Patricia, Ginger, Andrew, and Alex.

Plainly, much appreciation is owed the forty-three writers of the series' fifty-eight original essays; busy people who took time to share creative ideas and earnest feelings about our choices in making probable, possible, preferable, and preventable futures.

Several contributors (Glenn, Jeff, Joe, Josh, Marilyn, Nat, Roger, Sohail, and Tom) commented usefully on the essays of others. John Smart secured remarkable artwork for his two essays from Cris Dornaus. Marvin Cetron, Nat Irvin, Mel Konner, Robert Merikangas, and Patrick Salsbury ably adapted essays. Ann Coombs provided special research material of great value. While they did not write essays, Daniel Shostak did provide insightful discussion questions, as did

Nada Khader. Jacque Fresco and Roxanne Meadows shared their extraordinary artwork.

Many whose ideas are not aired directly in the book nevertheless made a vital contribution. Stevi Baggert, Connie Cordovilla, Judith Czigler, Alexander Friedlander, Thad McKenna, Adrienne Redd, and Emily Thorne helped recruit high school volunteers. Todd R. Grube identified editorial cartoons of high quality. Peggy Dominy, an Information Services Librarian at Drexel University, found hard-to-locate missing data. And, of course, there were many others whom I trust will forgive my regrettable memory lapse.

As before in the case of five books I edited in 2003/2004 on 9/11 and the Iraq War (DEFEATING TERRORISM/DEVELOPING DREAMS), the staff of Chelsea House did an especially fine job meeting some rather complex challenges, with special thanks going to the series editor, Christian Green.

For more than a quarter of a century, my wife, Lynn Seng, has contributed ideas of great value, reviews of keen insight, and support without which I would accomplish far less. Her belief in this project, and her love and smile, make all the difference.

Finally, I would like to acknowledge YOUR unique contribution, for it is ultimately only as you—and other readers—ponder and act on the book's many ideas that this volume can help us craft a world tomorrow that increasingly honors us all.

# Table of Contents

# Introduction

*Because we are here now, we are "on duty" and responsible for preserving the evolutionary integrity of the human experiment. We are the leaders we have been waiting for. We are the social innovators and entrepreneurs we have been seeking. We are the ones who are challenged to self-organize and pull ourselves up by our own bootstraps.*
—Duane Elgin,
*Promise Ahead*

Our focus in this second of our four volumes, *America: Moving Ahead*, is on some of the major choices ahead for our nation. Plainly, the sands are shifting under our feet. Attention is required to address turmoil in capitalism, employment, environmentalism, fundamentalism, globalism, militarism, stratification, and terrorism, among scores of such weighty matters.

Accordingly, we open Part One with a topic of special concern to high school students, namely, the likely world of work upon graduation and how to prepare. Among other questions our essayists ask is how important will a college diploma really be if seven of the top ten occupations with the greatest growth through 2012 will be in low-wage service fields requiring little education?[1]

To be sure, the pay premium for people with a college education continues to rise relative to workers without a degree, and earnings are only one among many significant returns on a college education (others include a sharper mind; more timely information; the example of learned, inquisitive role models; helpful friends; and possibly even nuggets of wisdom).[2] But, what if many college-level jobs are soon outsourced overseas? How can I best prepare for this possibility? (A consulting firm forecasts a loss by 2015 of 3,300,000 white-collar jobs to other countries.)[3]

Part Two focuses on four major areas of social problems—education, criminality, income maldistribution, and city life. The first essay imagines what K–12 schooling might include if and when we decide to make the most of information-technology possibilities. The second asks: Can we do a better job of reducing the toll of crime on victims and criminal alike? The third imagines what life for a teenager might resemble on the fiftieth anniversary of 9/11—a time when the United States may have made significant progress toward remedying inequities in income distribution. The fourth asks if we could use ocean-going ships to house large-scale experiments in a wide range of lifestyles, the better to afford us the choices we now only dream about.

Part Three shifts attention to the challenges involving the relationships we have with our neighbors around the planet (fellow passengers in lifeboat Earth). The first essay argues that we are better off for the "arrival" of globalization (actually a very old process), and we are urged to make the most of it. (Toys, for example, were 24 percent lower in price at Christmas 2003 than in 1997 because tariffs were lifted that year. While U.S. jobs have been lost, we are consumers as well as producers.)[4] The second essay approaches foreign relations from a different angle, albeit also a controversial one. The writer recommends that the United States employs its religious values (not dogma and practices) as guidelines for thought and behavior in foreign affairs. This is thought likely to help ensure the shaping of good law and policy.[5]

Part Four features forecasts about our war and peace prospects, topics with a strong link to ideas advanced in the preceding section. Special attention is paid to the Middle East, in general, and pragmatic solutions for its many problems, along with the situation in Iraq, in particular. Given the likelihood that by 2020 there may be more Muslims than Christians in the Western world, this emphasis would seem a sound one.[6] (Helpful here are five recent volumes of original essays I edited for this press in a series entitled DEFEATING TERRORISM/DEVELOPING DREAMS.)

Two final essays explain how peace can and must be promoted. The first insists that war, however ancient this brutish and stupid form of blood-letting, need *not* be part of our future. The second details varied field-tested steps for helping to make sure we war no more. Taken together they expand our horizons and give fresh hope.

The capstone essay with which the book closes boldly contends that you can rapidly (thirty seconds!) "take control and create your future, not drift into it." If, as a leading writer suggests, "the power to imagine is the first step in changing the world," the essays in this volume give us a strong start.[7]—Editor

NOTES

1  Steven Greenhouse, "If You're a Waiter, the Future Is Rosy," *New York Times*, 7 March 2004, wr-8.

2  Robert Reich, former secretary of labor, quoted in *Ibid*.

3  Forrester Research, cited in *Ibid*.

4  David Wesel, "Imports Help Consumers—If Not Politicos," *Wall Street Journal*, 25 March 2004, A2.

5  For a strong counterargument, see the Introduction to *Theater of War*, by Lewis Lapham (New York: The New Press, 2002).

6  Douglas Todd, "Explosive Trends for '04 and Beyond: Religion Faces Five Major Movements That Will Affect Everything from War to Sexuality," *Vancouver Sun*, 17 January 2004, C5.

7  Walter Mosely, "Black to the Future," in Marleen S. Barr, ed., *Envisioning the Future: Science Fiction and the Next Millennium* (Middletown, Conn.: Wesleyan University Press, 2003), 202. "The hardest thing is to break the chains of reality and go beyond into a world of your own creation." (204).

# Part One

## JOBS, CAREERS, AND WORKPLACES—TOMORROW

*I hear and I forget;*
*I see and I remember;*
*I do and I understand.*
—Chinese Proverb

America's teenagers have told pollsters that they intend to go after just about the same jobs year after year: They want to be teachers, computer field specialists, engineers, mechanics, doctors, musicians, nurses, and veterinarians (in that order of preference).[1] Specialists in labor market studies believe most, if not all, of these career lines will be substantially altered in the near future, if not by radical high-tech innovations (see, for example, the essay on K–12 schooling in Part Two), then by the incentive that companies have to send jobs overseas.

Accordingly, teenagers must increasingly ask: Will there be a good job for me when I go seeking it, whether after high school, college, the military, or whatever? Will there be good career lines, and several of them, as I change jobs seeking one (and then another one) more to my liking? What might I do to better prepare?

Essay One maps the contours of an increasingly strange landscape, the work world of tomorrow, and offers clues for successfully traversing it. The second essay forecasts greater-than-ever reliance on self-employment, and may be startling with its hard-nosed thoughts about college attendance. The third essay emphasizes the value of becoming a "wave-maker," while the fourth essay lays out the case for and against your becoming a doctor—or by careful extrapolation, a professional of any related kind—and urges all such professions to "reinvent themselves." The final essay takes a different tack altogether and tenders answers to the too-seldom-raised intriguing question: What might our future include if our labor movement had more sway?—Editor

## NOTE

1  George Gallup Jr., "Teens Aim for the Simple Things in Life," Gallup Poll, 6 January 2004. The actual study was completed from August 1 to 29, 2003. See also James Cooke Brown, *The Job Market of the Future: Using Computers to Humanize Economies* (Armonk, N.Y.: M.E. Sharpe, 2001). A creative case is made to replace the current labor market system with a computer-based one aimed at assuring all a quality job with a "living wage" or better. Helpful as well is Penn Kemble, ed., *Workforce Development and the New Unionism* (Washington, D.C.: New Economy Information Service, 2002). Its eleven essays explore how to "help strengthen the American economy and the labor movement at a moment when both can use it." (Morton Bahr, president, Communications Workers of America).

# FUTURE JOB TRENDS: PUZZLES, PITFALLS, AND PRIZES

### Jim Pinto
Technology Futurist

If you are going to get a good job in the near future, look to companies and technologies on the upswing. Major changes in work and careers will come in such fields as biotechnology, genetic engineering, nanotechnology, and space travel. Accordingly, I'll highlight below some especially challenging trends and some promising opportunities.

## JOB MIGRATION

Our population is expected to increase by a significant amount—24 million—from 2000 to 2010, which will mean more consumers of goods and services, spurring demand for workers in a wide range of occupations and industries.[1] This notwithstanding, many jobs are in line to permanently leave our shores soon—and you do not want to be at the losing end of that trend (Bisk, "The Future of Making a Living").

Analysts predict that by the next decade, several million white-collar jobs and almost $1 trillion in wages will shift from the United States to low-cost countries. The driving forces here are digitization, the Internet, and high-speed data networks that girdle the globe. Today, jobs that previously seemed truly leading edge, like designing a revolutionary microprocessor, can easily be performed overseas. That is why Intel and Texas Instruments are hiring Indian and Chinese engineers to design chips (Related Links D).

Bangalore (India), Manila (Philippines), Shanghai (China), Budapest (Hungary), and many other tech-centers in developing countries have become the new back office for Corporate

America, Corporate Japan, and Corporate Europe. Even Bulgaria, Romania, and South Africa, which have many educated people but remain economic backwaters, are tapping the global market for services.[2]

What makes this trend so viable is the explosion of (English-language proficient) college graduates in many low-wage nations. The Philippines, with a population of 75 million, churns out 380,000 college graduates each year, with an over-supply of accountants trained in U.S. accounting standards. India already has a staggering 520,000 information-technology engineers, with starting salaries of only around $5,000. American schools produce only 35,000 mechanical engineers a year; China graduates twice as many.

Engineers, accountants, and other professionals in the United States are headed for a tough readjustment. The trend in quantity of jobs and quality of financial rewards is clearly downward. Just two years ago, senior software engineers were paid up to $130,000 a year; the same jobs now pay less than $100,000. Computer help-desk jobs used to make about $55,000; now they get $30,000. The trend is spreading to virtually every kind of knowledge work.[3]

## JOBS THAT CANNOT SHIFT TO REMOTE LOCATIONS

Many jobs cannot go offshore because they require face-to-face contact with customers. We will continue to build homes and skyscrapers, deliver medical care, entertain one another, learn in classrooms, operate trains and planes, enjoy recreation together, negotiate deals, and audit local companies in a one-to-one, very personal way. Talented and innovative people—like you—will find fine jobs here, as they always have.

Inevitably, routine jobs that call for simply following policies and procedures will be shunted offshore, where cheaper labor is all that is required. But, it is an innovation-driven workforce that will continue to generate productivity growth. The companies that succeed in this new age will be those that understand how to combine and coordinate new organizations and new thinking in the real-time environment.

Routine work will decline in value—the work of sewing machine and telephone operators, travel agents, etc. At the same time, opportunities will multiply for those who are flexible, creative, and good with people. Complex jobs and work that involves motivating and coordinating people will flourish—educators, managers, consultants, artists, and designers (Related Links B).

Some analysts (including myself) think that the United States will see a net gain from this ongoing job shift—as with previous globalization waves (for example, we gave up making steel in the 1970s, and today import ever finer and cheaper steel from abroad). The U.S. labor force and capital will be redeployed to higher-value industries and cutting-edge research and development. Silicon Valley gurus are already talking about the next wave of U.S. innovation coming from the fusion of software, nanotech, and life sciences. The waves of change can and should continue to increase the levels of productivity and value, with resulting gains for all of us.

### THE PRODUCTIVITY RACE

Productivity has now become a global race, an international competition between regions and nations for the single reason that it is the source of the wealth, the key to improvements in living standards. Those who can make things cheaper, faster, better—win!

Today, real-time applications are becoming widespread. Web services allow integration and delivery of real-time information to all parts of the enterprise. Low-cost, effective applications are available that allow cooperating suppliers and users to monitor, analyze, optimize, and adjust business processes in real time.

The drive for real-time operations and services is reshaping business today. The resulting productivity boost is generating startling results. Indeed, this is perhaps the key factor behind the so-called jobless recovery. It is not that jobs are being eliminated by automation, or going offshore. It is just that many jobs have simply disappeared, eliminated by productivity improvements (*Business Week*, 3 February 2003).

*Business Week* estimates that a 1 percent productivity improvement can eliminate up to 1.3 million jobs. With productivity growing at an annual rate of 3 to 5 percent, the reason for the jobs shortfall becomes clear.[4] Of the 2.7 million jobs lost over the last three years, only 300,000 have been from outsourcing, according to Forrester Research.[5]

### TOMORROW'S OFFICE JOBS

This is the age of the knowledge worker. Over the next ten to twenty years, skilled jobs will be on the rise as never before. They will proliferate in nursing, computer science, entertainment, financial services, and entirely new fields that may still be just a gleam in the eyes of the innovators. So, today's teens will have enormous opportunities for challenging and creative careers.

The OfficeTeam Career Center lists the following office-type job titles, showing functions that may increase in importance in the coming decade. They are based on in-depth interviews with internal offices worldwide as well as other technology and workplace experts. The list includes either individual job titles or growing functions within broader titles (Related Links J).

* Staffing Strategist; Manager of Strategic Innovation; Mentoring Director;
* Internet Strategist; Fitness Manager; Director of Wellness; Information Coordinator;
* Catering Manager; Communications Facilitator; Career Coach; Telecommuting Coordinator; Business Etiquette Advisor/Consultant.

There are many things that you can do within these emerging job titles to make sure that you, and the company you work for, remain competitive. Become proactive, more of a salesman and marketer. Go with the sales people to visit customers; find out what they need for you to be competitive. Help the marketers write the specifications for new products. Find new ways to shorten development cycles and reduce production time frames. Look for ways and means to do things faster, cheaper and better, using superior tools and new technologies. Think ahead, not back. Look to lead, not follow.

## TOMORROW'S JUICY HIGH-TECH JOBS

Historically, job growth has come through a surge of new, innovative high-tech areas. Unlike during the 1990s, when new information technologies boomed, no new industries have emerged in the early years of the new century. But the opportunities are coming. *Business Week* (see references) suggests that these are the fields that will create the juicy jobs in the next decade:

* Telecom—Broadband and wireless technologies will bring new jobs in animation, video, and other forms of "rich media."
* Biotech—The results of the decoding of the human genome have led to many new start-up biotechnology companies. Many of these are the new giants of tomorrow.
* Nanotech—Advances in atomic level devices and new forms of manufacturing are bringing a new surge of start-ups, attracting experts in computer science, basic materials, and applied physics.
* Energy—The drive to develop economic alternatives to oil will create many new jobs in fields like solar power and hydrogen fuel cells, as well as in the new infrastructure that will be needed for these activities. There will be tremendous new growth in electric power, new types of automobiles, and the manufacturing of related new products.
* Space—The long-awaited commercialization of space will open up new frontiers and new jobs. Entrepreneurs will come up with new opportunities like space tourism and the mining of asteroids.

## WHAT TO LOOK FOR

A recent article in *IEEE Spectrum* described ten of the coolest, baddest, hippest, grooviest (depending on your generation), most gratifying engineering jobs in the world. The criterion was simple—find the people having the most fun. The article zeroed in on jobs involving a deep connection with technology (Related Links D).

Dave Fruehling was profiled sitting in a soundproof studio, jamming on a classic electric guitar. John Gage was in Beijing, hanging out at a university and practicing his Chinese. Steve Sullivan was on a movie set or tweaking the performance of a virtual actor. Karl Stahlkopf was found on a Hawaiian beach, pondering the waves and the wind. Lau Kofoed Kierstein was sitting on the floor with a few six-year-old boys, playing with action figures. Sounds like fun? Of course. But, for these electrical engineers, it is also work, just a part of their jobs. Look for a job that you'll enjoy—and you'll find it.

## DISCRIMINATION AND THE GENDER GAP

As the global village becomes a true mixture of people of different races, creeds, and national origin, discrimination of any sort will steadily become a thing of the past. In business, the brightest and the best—the people who get results—will have the best opportunities.

Even though many women hold top jobs in business, it is somewhat strange that there is still a gender gap in the United States and most otherwise advanced countries. There is less of one in China and some third-world countries, where pay and prospects appear to be gender-neutral—though it is evident that the top political and business positions are still overwhelmingly dominated by men. As time progresses, this will slowly and inexorably become less evident, though cultural biases will affect progress.

During the last several decades, as women gained traction in the workforce, gender differences turned up in every workplace, from offices to factory floors to military positions. Now women are pulling up chairs at boardroom tables and launching their own companies—the number of woman-owned firms has increased more than 100 percent in the last decade, and the trend will continue.

In the United States, many women prefer to get sidetracked into staff jobs, with the home and family more important than upward job mobility. If you are a creative and assertive woman, your opportunities are significant. More and more CEOs of major corporations are women, and many people think that women make better CEOs and political leaders than men— they tend to avoid adversarial situations and instead look for compromise and win-win possibilities (Related Links E). Perhaps the United States will even have a woman president within the next decade.

### MULTIPLE CAREERS

With medical advances, human life expectancy may increase at the rate of ten years every ten years. Strange as this may sound, thirty years from now, you can expect to live to well over one hundred, far longer than the current expected life span of seventy to eighty years. The world will have an increasing number of older and healthier people. Because of this shift, retirement age will inevitably be postponed well beyond the current sixty-five years—already being increased to seventy years and beyond.[6]

A person's working career will extend from the present average of forty years, to perhaps sixty or more. So, don't expect to have just one career path—you will inevitably move to different kinds of jobs during different phases of your life. It is like tennis or baseball players who have to do something else after their prowess has waned. Besides, wouldn't it be boring just to be an engineer, or a teacher, all your life? Life seems more exciting when you can consider working at the many different things that you enjoy.

### THE GLOBAL VILLAGE

Consider offshore capabilities as resources to be used to help your company become stronger. Ask your company if you can visit China, India, or Singapore to broaden your own scope and vision. Find out how remote capabilities can reduce costs and shorten development time frames. Seek out the ways and means to complement and maximize your own results.[7]

## SUMMARY

Tomorrow's work world promises to challenge young job-seekers in novel and often bewildering ways. Focus on jobs that are trending upward. Above all, don't fall into the trap of taking the first job that comes along, only to find out too late that it is part of a declining trend.[8] The sooner you look over the job horizon, the better your chances—and those of our nation—of enjoying our rapidly changing work world.

NOTES

1  This means a slightly faster rate of growth than during the 1990–2000 period but slower than the 1980–90 period. The youth population, age 16 to 24, will grow more rapidly than the overall population, a turnaround that began in the mid-1990s. As the baby boomers continue to age, the 55-to-64 age group will increase by 11 million people over the 2000–10 period—more than any other group. Those age 35 to 44 will be the only group to decrease in size, reflecting the birth dearth that followed the baby boom. Minorities and immigrants will constitute a larger share of the U.S. population in 2010 than they do today. Minority groups that have grown the fastest in the recent past—Hispanics and Asians and others—are projected to continue to grow much faster than white, non-Hispanics.

2  Many European countries' birthrates are already as low as 1.5, with Germany and Italy around 1.3. Half the population in Germany (the world's number three economy) will soon be over 65. At the current rate, Italy, now with about 60 million people, will have 20 million by the latter part of this century. India is the world's largest democracy, with a population now exceeding 1 billion. Its birthrate, which is not controlled like China's, exceeds 3.3, and this means that India will have the

world's largest population, overtaking China midway through the century.

3  Virtually every sector of the financial industry is undergoing a similar revolution. Processing insurance claims, selling stocks, and analyzing companies can all be done in Asia for one-third to one-half the cost in the United States or Europe. Wall Street investment banks and brokerages, under mounting pressure to offer independent research to investors, are buying equity analysis, industry reports, and summaries of financial disclosures from financial analysts in India. By mining Web databases, off-shore staff in Delhi or Prague can scrutinize credit histories, access corporate financial disclosures, and troll oceans of economic statistics. Even Wall Street jobs paying $80,000 are getting easier to transfer; big brokerages are starting to use Indian financial analysts for number-crunching work.

4  James Cooper, "The Price of Efficiency," *Business Week*, 22 March 2004, 38.

5  *Ibid.*

6  There should be plenty of work for older people, too. Fifty years ago, my grandfather looked old and feeble at sixty. Today, the official retirement age of sixty-five seems absurd, as active life in developed countries extends to seventy-five and beyond. Within the next decade, the ground rules for retirement will change drastically, and the official retirement age will be post-poned, causing older people to remain in the workforce. For several years now, Wal-Mart has been hiring older people as "greeters," reflecting the need for customers to feel welcome as they enter the store. Beyond that, increasing numbers of retired people will want productive employment, and will take jobs that reflect their experience and value to the enterprise. Home Depot has started employing seniors in supporting jobs, and this trend will extend to more involved and rewarding employment for senior citizens.

7  You can help our nation maintain our lead in technology innovation. This means promoting a strong national commitment to investment in research and development, plus continued stimulation of a world-leading education and business infrastructure, which the world recognizes as the basis of our leadership.

8  When you have completed your schooling, don't stop—continue

with a lifetime of learning. No matter what type of work you do in the future, keep looking for ways to improve it, to stay abreast of the changes that will inevitably occur. Develop the attitude of leadership during times of change. The best advice I can give is to welcome change, expect the unexpected. Don't resist change—drive it and use it to improve yourself and the world.

## REFERENCES

Bisk, Tsvi. "The Future of Making a Living." (Essay Two in this volume)

Coombs, Ann with Malcolm Morgan. "Innovating the Future." (Essay Three in this volume)

Drucker, Peter. *Managing in the Next Society*. New York: Truman Talley Books, 2002. The management guru covers technology and society trends, emerging industries, and management and sociological changes. He tracks U.S. business movement away from manufacturing to service and distribution, with new discussions on emerging biotechnology and knowledge management. Drucker provides valuable insights into a fast-changing society, and his depth and wisdom shine through. This easy-to-read book will help you gain a broad perspective on the changes that are flooding this new century.

———. *Management Challenges for the 21st Century*. New York: HarperBusiness, 2001. Includes new and revolutionary ideas and perspectives on the central management issues of the new century by the most important management thinker of our time. Born in 1909, Drucker is more than ever incisive, challenging, and mind-stretching. This new book is forward-looking and forward-thinking.

Moody, Patricia, and Richard Morley. *The Technology Machine: How Manufacturing Will Work in the Year 2020*. New York: Free Press, 1999. Richard Morley is the inventor of the programmable logic controller (PLC), now housed in the Smithsonian Institution. He is a founder or cofounder of more than ten companies. Moody and Morley supply simple guidelines for future growth and detail their vision for future systems, leaders, and workers.

"The New Global Job Shift," *Business Week*, 3 February 2003. Excellent discussion of job trends and the problem of jobs lost by outsourcing to low-wage countries.

"Where Are the Jobs? The Future of Work," *Business Week*, 22 March 2004. A complete section reviews the "jobless recovery" and suggests that job losses are coming more from productivity increases than foreign outsourcing.

## WEB SITES

A) U.S. Department of Labor (Bureau of Labor Statistics)—Tomorrow's jobs. Important overview regarding what will happen to jobs in the next decade. http://www.bls.gov/oco/oco2003.htm.

B) "Hottest Careers in IT." Infotech-related jobs are creating new avenues to building careers. http://supplements.inq7.net/managingit/display.php?fld=vir&art=vir02.htm. http://ph.jobstreet.com/career/streetwise/techtalk13.htm.

C) "The Enterprise of the 21$^{st}$ Century." Seven technology-fueled trends will change the shape of organizations in the new Knowledge Age. http://www.destinationkm.com/articles/default.asp?ArticleID=79.

D) "IEEE—Engineering Dream Jobs 2004." Discusses the dreams of ten engineers. Insights into what could be your dream job. http://www.spectrum.ieee.org/WEBONLY/publicfeature/feb04/0204job.html.

E) "Why Women Make Better Managers." Good discussion on an important subject. Presents cogent arguments as to why women have the edge. http://www.mime.eng.utoledo.edu/people/faculty/rbennett/womenmanagers.htm.

F) "Donald Norman Looks Forward to the New Century." Excellent broad discussion on the significant changes that will occur in the new century. http://www.jnd.org/dn.mss/MITPressTheFuture.html.

G) U.S. Department of Labor (Bureau of Labor Statistics)—Chart showing the percentage change in wage and salary employment, service-providing industry divisions, 1992–2002 and projected 2002–2012: http://www.bls.gov/oco/images/ocotjc04.gif.

H) U.S. Department of Labor (Bureau of Labor Statistics)—Chart showing the percentage change in wage and salary employment, goods-producing industry divisions, 1992–2002 and projected 2002–2012: http://www.bls.gov/oco/images/ocotjc05.gif.

I) "The Future of Work"—interesting and helpful British Web site: http://www.leeds.ac.uk/esrcfutureofwork/.

J) OfficeTeam.com describes job titles that portray functions that may increase in importance in the coming years. The list includes either individual job titles or growing functions within broader titles: http://www.officeteam.com/OT/TopJobTitles.

## ■ Essay Two ■

# THE FUTURE OF MAKING A LIVING

Tsvi Bisk

Futurist/Strategy Analyst

What's happening? Well, in the time it will take you to read this essay more changes will have probably occurred in the world than would have in a week (or even a month) only a hundred years ago. Accordingly, in the world of work, everything is in flux—at a speed and in a depth that outdoes anything seen to date.

There is little surprise then that the life span of a successful Fortune 500 company (the 500 largest companies in the world) is now forty years or half that of a human being. (Bonnici) Or that one-third of the Fortune 500 companies listed in 1970 disappeared by 1983. (Merry and Daniels) Small U.S. companies have an even shorter shelf life: 98 percent disappear within eleven years of their founding; 70 percent within eight years of their founding; and 50 percent within four years of their founding (Daniels). The average life span of all companies in Japan and Europe is a little more than twelve years (Bonnici and Daniels).

The hearse of history is on its way to pick up the body of yesteryear's staid employment model (become a college graduate, get a job with a big corporation or in the civil service, work dutifully for forty years, and retire with a modest pension). This model is in "intensive care" and will soon be declared incurable.

### CHANGES IN JOB PROFILE
We are speeding up a long-term change in the distribution of jobs. According to the U.S. Department of Commerce, about

31

80 percent of Americans in 1820 made their living as farmers while less than 2 percent do today. In 1947, according to the Federal Reserve Bank of Chicago, about 35 percent of America's workforce was employed in manufacturing (*The Economist*). Today the figure is 12 to 14 percent (*The Economist* and *Fortune*).

From 1995 to 2002, the world's twenty largest economies lost 22 million industrial jobs. Of these, the United States lost about 2 million industrial jobs and China (where all these jobs are supposed to be going) lost 15 million manufacturing jobs (*Fortune*). Robots are replacing humans or are greatly enhancing human performance in mining, manufacturing, and even agriculture. Huge areas of clerical work are also being automated. Standardized repetitive work is being taken over by robots.

Despite the shrinking of the United States' industrial workforce, the country's overall industrial output has increased by an astonishing 50 percent since 1992 (*The Economist*). The key to the United States' continued prosperity depends on shifting to ever more productive and diverse services. And the good news is that jobs here are often better paying and far more interesting than those we knew on the farms and the assembly line.

**CHANGES IN SCALE**

Because of this, the United States is relying more and more on smaller rather than larger companies. There is now one company for every seven workers. It is estimated that by 2020 there will be one company for every three workers. Ninety percent of the new "jobs" (work opportunities) are being created by companies with less than twenty workers, many of whom are not salaried and are part time or temporary (Pink, 39).

The smaller the company, the less it can do by itself, and the more it must contract out, often to an even smaller company. In addition, consumers of services must be dealt with individually. Smaller companies have a flexibility that large companies, used to dealing with mass markets, do not have. Opportunities for mini-entrepreneurs serving small-niche markets are growing at the speed of light. High schoolers can expect to find numerous job opportunities after graduation providing services to these small companies.

## EMERGENCE OF SELF-EMPLOYMENT

Future historians will identify the twentieth century as the first *and* last in which most people in the working population were salaried employees. As the twenty-first century progresses, the very character of the postindustrial economy will force more and more people into self-employment. This is already occurring at such a rapid rate it might be called a revolution. In 1998, 22 percent of the workforce in the United States was self-employed; by 2000, the figure was 26 percent (Pink, 34). While this transformation might not continue at the same uniform high rate, one thing seems certain—it will continue, until most of the workforce is self-employed.

Millions of companies actually consist of only one person. Indeed, 69 percent of the companies starting up every year in the United States are being established in the home (Pink, 40). These new home-based service companies avoid salaried workers like the plague. They would rather make less profit than establish a traditional employer-employee relationship. Instead, when their business expands—if ever—they network with another self-employed service provider or they hire contract labor from a manpower company.

## AGE OF THE SELF-EMPLOYED

A growing number of people have a "portfolio" of various kinds of income-generating occupations. For example, I work two days a week as a part-time salaried translator for a large public institution. I am also a junior partner in an incorporated translation company (which is really a two-man show run out of our respective homes). I teach history part time for a private school. I give lectures and workshops on the study of the future (theory and practice), and I periodically give "Work Search" workshops as a subcontractor for a contractor who has won government work in this area. We "portfolio workers" may already be the fastest growing class in the modern work market.

How can you prepare for the Age of the Self-Employed? It is likely that you will have five to seven careers in your lifetime and fifteen to twenty places of work (*not* jobs). Where preparation is concerned, the old order of importance used to be formal education, skills, experience, and personal attributes. Today, the new order is just the reverse—personal attributes, skills, experience, and formal education.

In a work world in which you will have to change careers many times, your formal education, your experience, and even your skills will become repeatedly obsolete. Your personal attributes are what will keep you fit for the job market, and they especially include the ability to teach yourself new skills, the ability to manage yourself, the ability to work with people, and a healthy dose of creativity and imagination.

Unfortunately, very little in your schooling until now has been devoted to encouraging you to develop these attributes. In fact, much of your schooling has been dedicated to undermining the development of such attributes. Because of this you will have to teach yourselves how to cultivate and develop them. I suggest you read as many biographies of successful people as possible. Make the reading of biographies your hobby. Also, when you surf the Internet, go to as many biography Web sites as possible and read them for your own enjoyment.

**WHAT ABOUT HIGHER EDUCATION?**
Well, if you know what you want to do and it is a technical profession (doctor, engineer, lawyer, etc.), get into the most affordable school you can for your bachelor's degree. A bachelor's degree today is as valuable in the work market as a high school diploma was fifty years ago. It makes no sense to spend more than $100,000 for such a credential. It makes much more sense to save your money for your graduate degree or professional credential.

But what if you don't know what you want to do, and you still want to go to college (or your parents would be disappointed if you didn't)? Well, current statistics show that education of any sort is still a good investment. People with college degrees earn, on average, 50 percent more than people without one during the course of their working lives.

But it is not what you have learned that is important; it is the fact that you have shown the ability to earn a degree. This indicates a certain level of intelligence, learning ability, discipline, and communications skills, which still means something in the current employment market. Whether it will continue to mean something given what I have cited above is not certain.

The most affordable way to get the degree is as follows: go to a community or junior college to earn your associate degree (sixty credits)—two-year colleges are the cheapest way to earn credits. Get work experience during this time, as much as your energy and schedule allow. Strive to finish in the top tenth of your class. Transfer these sixty credits into a branch of your local and inexpensive state university.

Or, conversely, explore the possibility of a regionally accredited for-profit college or university (Bisk). These are particularly student friendly, reasonably priced, and totally geared to today's work market. Make sure that the state university or for-profit institution will accept all your two-year college credits before you even begin the process. Save your money for a good graduate school if you desire to earn a higher degree.

This strategy can be made to look very positive on your resume or in an interview with a prospective employer or client. Simply remember and repeat in your own words that (a) it is foolish to invest a lot of money in a bachelor's degree; (b) earning your degree at several institutions gave you a wider perspective; (c) the ability to work while studying is just as much a part of the learning process as the formal studies; and (d) controlling your learning strategy in this way helped you develop the attributes cited above: initiative, creativity, and self-reliance.

### ON NOT GETTING A HIGHER DEGREE

If you are not academically inclined (and this has nothing to do with intelligence), you should welcome the age of the self-employed. If this is a self-esteem problem for you, remember that such models of economic success as Bill Gates, Steven Jobs, Steven Spielberg, and Larry Ellison do not have a bachelor's degree. Thomas Edison, among scores of yesteryear's luminaries, did not even finish elementary school.

First, disabuse yourself of the notion that you need a university education to survive and prosper in the age of the self-employed. Outside of specialized technical and professional tasks (engineers, doctors), the requirement for an academic credential is often an artificial one.[1] I believe the courts may soon begin to rule against its use.[2]

The "service economy" is a boon to the nonacademically inclined. Finding a reliable, quality car mechanic, electrician, floor-covering installer, glazier, painter, or plumber is probably more difficult today than finding a reliable, quality brain or plastic surgeon. Many of these blue-collar jobs are also recession-proof occupations. You may experience a slight decline in income during a full-blown recession, but you will never be unemployed (if you are reliable). When the car does not start, the fuse blows, or the toilet overflows, you will get the call no matter what the state of the economy, and this will be true in 2010, 2020, and so on.

I have very serious doubts about robotics replacing service workers of this kind. Duplicating the inherent mental flexibility of human beings will be economically prohibitive for a long time to come. For a robot to ask—"What does your car sound like when you start it on a cold morning?"—and to understand your answer is really a long way off.

**CONCLUSION**

Get used to the idea that you will probably not have a salaried job to go to every day, one steady job for life. Instead, you will probably constantly look for contract work. Consider becoming a portfolio worker (one who works at several different "jobs" in any one period). Develop the fortitude, optimism, and creativity necessary to prevail in a self-employed economy. Seek a healthy balance of work and home life. And enjoy learning new job-related skills and cultivating the dynamic joy of existence.

### ADDENDA: IMPACT ON LABOR UNIONS

Given this rejection of the traditional employer-employee relationship, the age of long-term employment in one job is dead, as is the union-bargained labor contract for a mass of wage earners. Both the giant corporation's "Organization Man" and the unionized hourly or salaried worker characterized the twentieth century. Now, the self-employed portfolio worker, the mini-entrepreneur, and the small business owner will characterize the twenty-first century.

Accordingly, labor unions face a very uncertain future. Civil service employees in federal, state, and local government are an example—probably the last such one—of a workplace where full-time, unionized salaried workers are the rule. In the private sector, the Teamsters and the building trades unions, as well as a few others, still wield a lot of clout. But even here we will probably soon witness employers turning to outsourcing to self-employed subcontractors—driven by the lower-priced example of nonunionized industry and office services.

This development will spell the end of unions as we have known them in the industrial era. Those who cannot evolve will become extinct. Some unions will evolve into guilds and associations to protect the rights and interests of the self-employed portfolio worker and the mini-entrepreneur. These will survive.

NOTES
_____

1  Peter Drucker, the famous management guru, once cited a study comparing the bank workers of Montreal, who did not need an academic credential, to the bank workers of Toronto, who did. The study found absolutely no difference in performance, efficiency, or service to the client. The academic credential has come to function as a preliminary filter for the

personnel directors of big companies and the regulation writers of the civil service. It makes life easier for the bureaucrats of the private and the public sectors.

2  Nonacademic professional associations have also begun to make an academic credential a prerequisite in order to limit competition (always with "grandfather clauses" excusing the veteran members of the association from this prerequisite). I predict that in the near future the courts in the United States will be asked to rule on the constitutionality of this practice, especially in cases where a formal state license is required to practice a certain profession.

The *needless* use (and I stress needless because there are countless areas where an academic credential *is* needed) of the academic credential as a prerequisite to getting work has had two very negative effects. First, it is undemocratic and anti-meritocracy in that it closes off ever growing areas of work from the poorer classes whose inferior schooling has not prepared them for university.

Second, it has resulted in a lowering of standards at our universities and a cheapening of the academic credential. This is because hordes of young people not temperamentally suited or scholastically prepared for academic life have been seeking an academic credential, and universities and colleges have been forced over time to accommodate their lower academic capabilities.

## REFERENCES

Bisk, Tsvi. www.adultdegree.com.

Bonnici, Tanya Sammut. www.refresher.com/!eternity

Colvin, Geoffrey. "Worrying about Jobs Isn't Productive." *Fortune Magazine*. 10 November 2003, 29.

Daniels, Barrington. www.lifeworkassociates.co.uk.

Merry, Uri. www.learning-org.com/98.04/0158.html.

"The Misery of Manufacturing." *The Economist*. 27 September 2003, 25–26.

Naisbitt, John. *Global Paradox*. New York: Avon Books, 1995.

Pink, Daniel H. *Free Agent Nation*. New York: Warner Books, 2001.

*"Somewhere out there, Patrick, is the key to increased sales. I want
you to find that key, Patrick, and bring it to me."*

# INNOVATING THE FUTURE

## Ann Coombs
President, Coombs Consulting, Ltd.

with

## Malcolm Morgan
Writer/Journalist

Who are our young "rulebreakers," "rebels," and "change drivers?" Young people admired for helping to forge a finer future? Their ranks, large and diverse, include Shania Twain, a musician who brought a rock sound to country music, something truly innovative and unique. She presents herself more inventively on stage and in music videos than most other country stars. Eminem, for another, excels at hip-hop, a form of music usually dominated by African American recording artists.

Consider as well the *Star Wars* couple, actors Natalie Portman and Hayden Christensen, who play Queen Amidala and Anakin Skywalker. Both began acting in theater and movies while children, and managed high school while pursuing stellar careers on stage and screen. Natalie now attends Harvard while making movies in her spare time.

You do not have to be a performer, however, to make your own way, to go against the norm to realize your "gift." But you do have to resist others who would stop you with negative appraisals of your character or potential.

So, who else can be this type of wave-making person? Kathleen Haley is from Riverside County, California. As a high schooler, she wanted to be a writer and journalist. When Kathleen went to high school (for her first two years at Riverside Poly High School, for her junior and senior years at San Gorgonio High School), she developed her liberal progressive political views. These included supporting civil liberties for disadvantaged groups, concentrating mainly on Latino immigrants to the United States. She was inspired by the contrast between the views and experiences of the white, conservative Republican population at Riverside Poly High and the Latino majority at San Gorgonio.

Kathleen was concerned that not all citizens in the United States started on a level playing field, in the workforce as well as in American society in general. She joined the American Civil Liberties Union when she was sixteen. She protested California's 1994 initiative, Proposition 187, intended to limit social services for illegal immigrants in California, and she wrote a poem for the ACLU criticizing Republican Newt Gingrich, speaker of the House of Representatives during the 1995–96 anti-immigrant 104th Congress.

In 2004, President George W. Bush won passage of a law granting Permanent Resident cards to some Latinos working in the United States illegally, without regular employee rights and benefits. Kathleen saw the need for this kind of measure several years earlier while still a teenager. Highly innovative in her thinking, she used her efforts to promote these ideas while still in high school.

But, as in the cases of most innovators, Kathleen was judged harshly by those surrounding her—most immediately by her peers at Riverside Poly, who labeled her a soft-hearted and soft-headed liberal, a weirdo. Only adults also in favor of civil liberties gave her any approval.

That didn't stop Kathleen. She faced opposition fearlessly and resisted conforming to the norm in order to push her ideas forward. Today, she knows she will always be involved with social issues, and she sees herself engaging people in social issues and using her writing to contribute to social, cultural, and political change. She now attends graduate school in journalism at the University of British Columbia, in Vancouver, Canada, and writes creatively in her spare time. She has pursued her ambitions courageously, even going to another country so that she could use her talents to reach her dreams.

### AND YOU?

What opportunities are there for *you* to be innovative? Ask yourself what activities, causes, or pursuits are important to you? What are your great ideas? What are your dreams? How can you bring these things to actuality, using your talents? (Have you even identified what your talents and interests are?)

In the larger scope, you can then ask, what changes are needed in society and in the world? What would a preferable future look and feel like? What would you have to do to help advance some of the many requisite changes? How could you draw on your distinctive personal resources (talents and intelligence)?

For example, a given high school student, call him Jacob, may realize he is good at math—at wrestling with complex mathematical problems. He dreams of furthering knowledge in the field, helping to find new solutions to important mathematical problems, and constructing ever deeper problems that may lead to still greater knowledge. What are the paths in and after high school he could possibly take to realize his dream?

Or another high school student, call her Mingmei, discovers that she is good at and loves the social sciences. She dreams of finding new ways to help make social institutions, like the public school system she has almost graduated from, far more beneficial for all the people in it—students, teachers, administrators, and staff. What steps could she take—while still in high school and for decades afterward? What type of environment— personal, political, spiritual, and physical—should she seek if she is to meet her goal?

By getting some hypothetical practice, that is, by wrestling mentally with the questions that high schoolers like Jacob and Mingmei have to address, you can begin your own path to innovation. And you don't have to be afraid to mix it up and do things differently. That's what innovators are known for doing.

### ACTION STEPS

As for "getting there from here," you could head for the hills and get out of your usual surroundings. There is nothing like a rock climb for gaining a new perspective. Figuratively, drop your pens and go for the crayons—color inspires. Get unrealistic—there is nothing wrong with asking the "what if" and "why not" questions, and not just following the normal and safe route of inquiry.

You might want to try "mind-mapping," a technique that has you choose to start at the middle of the page instead of the top left hand corner and seeing where you go from there. With this technique, your thoughts set the course in brainstorming fashion; you reject the idea of an outline and just put down a word, short phrase, or symbol on the page, circle it, build outward, and watch for connections and unfolding possibilities.

When you dare to go through a creative self-discovery process, including using techniques like getting unrealistic, you will probably find that you are thinking and acting in fresh and challenging ways. You will be on the cutting edge of the near future. Career-wise, you may help lead people in your field, shape the way it is practiced, and help lead it into completely new territory.

Every advance in any field, be it music, medicine, social justice, politics, or sports, has happened initially because of the individual drive of one self-aware, boldly planning, and implementing innovator—often a fairly young person. Without such people, fields in which we see greatness and invention would not have turned out that way.

Today, at the outset of the twenty-first century, there is a talent revolution in the works, and high school and college-age people are at the forefront. Future societies, if they are to prove open to advancement, will welcome, foster, and really understand the innovative skills of certain emerging practitioners. Ideally, the world will help young change-agents flourish.

To reiterate: If you would like to be an innovator, you must first be inspired and form your own novel ideas and vision. You must cultivate your own distinctive talents and interests. You must be prepared to go against the norm in the process. And you must expect to face opposition without backing down or compromising your basic values.

With this clear, it might help to take a Self-Discovery Quiz: *Are you yet an Innovator?*

1) Would you consider at least some of your ideas creative, fresh, and constructive?

2) Do you stand out from your peers because of these ideas?

3) Do such ideas lead you to behave in a manner that leads others to admire you and/or be inspired by you?

4) Do you have a solid idea of the deepest essence of who you are and an idea of what your role in society could or should be?

5) Do you have knowledge, talents, skills, and/or visions that you want to contribute to your society's betterment?

6) Do you feel you can transcend difficulties in order to make this contribution?

7) Can you see yourself using your knowledge, skills, talent, and/or visions to play a significant role in your society's (or the world's) future?

8) Finally, do you see yourself as a potentially powerful actor in your society, possibly capable of helping soon to make innovative changes, or not?

A positive answer to several of these questions suggests that you are on your way to being an inspiring rulebreaker and/or thought-leader in the near future. Having many negative answers is no cause for alarm—and may give you the impetus to reconsider your notion of yourself. For it is only through your own efforts that inspiring dreams can help create a finer reality, a finer near future.

* All individual references made in this essay are to actual people, except for the hypothetical student references, Jacob and Mingmei.

FURTHER READING

Corwin, Miles. *And Still We Rise: The Trials and Triumphs of Twelve*

*Gifted Inner-City High School Students*. New York: William & Morrow, 2000. This is a true account of one teacher's class of advanced-placement students at Crenshaw High School in inner-city Los Angeles. Despite being in a difficult, violent, impoverished area, they strive for success against all odds, and win.

Dickerson, James L. *Natalie Portman: Queen of Hearts*. Toronto: ECW Press, 2002. This biography explores the influences and ambitions, career, home life, and personal side of the young woman who is famous while only in her early twenties and has acted alongside major Hollywood stars in several films.

Harrill, Suzanne E. *Empowering Teens to Build Self-Esteem*. Castle Rock, Colo.: Innerworks Publishing, 1993. This is a practical guide that shows young people how to overcome negative self-images, and encourages them to take responsibility for their choices and take control of their lives. The author touches on eight principles of self-esteem, forty affirmations, dating tips, and journal questions for peer pressure.

## WEB SITES

www.idea-a-day.co.uk

Great site for inspiration and building upon your innovative ideas.

www.bytesforlife.com

Positive thinking strategies.

www.smith.edu/newssmith/NSFall99/achievers.html

"High Achievers Recall Their Epiphanies."

www.rediff.com/us/2000/mar/24us3.htm

"Amazing Success Story of a Teen Techie."

## ■ Essay Four ■

# CARE TO BE A DOCTOR TOMORROW?

Sohail Inayatullah, Ph.D.

*Editor, Journal of Futures Studies*

By 2020, will doctors have become "knowledge navigators," helping patients made glassy-eyed by "health advice" Web sites judge what is gold and what is junk?[1] How likely is it that patients—you and I—will have switched from today's conventional care routines to alternative therapies, like chiropractic, acupuncture, and meditation? Will our family doctor even be needed as dramatic technological advances—with such strange names as pharmacogenomics and nanotechnology—gain the power to actually repair defective genes?

Seven trends are transforming a doctor's future (and ours, as well): globalization, the Internet revolution, the genetics revolution, the pharmacogenomics revolution, the nanotech revolution, alternative medicine, and aging. The first two are full-blown trends while the latter five are emerging and can create futures unrecognizable to us today.

### GLOBALIZATION

This ongoing change can lead to faster access to news and technological breakthroughs elsewhere (true for doctors as well as patients). And it is a direct challenge to the idea of universal coverage. Whether for ideological reasons (privatization or market forces are represented as more efficient and better able to meet customers' needs) or for cost reasons (aging of the population, medicalization of illnesses), universal health care, as achieved in advanced OECD (Organization for Economic Cooperation and Development) nations, is under serious threat.

## THE INTERNET REVOLUTION

Working in tandem with globalization, indeed, accelerating this process is the dot-com revolution. While currently Web-based, it will probably soon lead to always-on, wearable computers, or Web-bots. Emergent health-bots may take a robotic form or a more virtual form—either a robodoc or an always-present (24/7) doctors.com-type Web site.

As the Web develops, we can anticipate health-bots, or health coaches. They should be able to provide individualized, immediate feedback; for example, letting us know the caloric intake of the pizza we just ate and the amount of exercise needed to burn it off. They will probably also let us know the makeup of each product we are considering purchasing, helping us to identify allergies and safeguarding us against them. Sensors may soon be developed that will be able to detect health problems through the smell of our breath, and alert doctors for early diagnosis and response.

These computer systems will be reflexive knowledge systems, endlessly learning more and more about us—our preferred and not so preferred internal and external environment. What is crucial is that these bots will be customized, immediate, and reflexive—that is, connected and learning, and individualized.

The health futurist Clement Bezold writes: "In 2010, our DNA profile will be part of our electronic medical record, and our genetically based proclivity to major diseases, including heart disease, will be known. There will be sophisticated, low-cost, noninvasive or minimally invasive biomonitoring devices; for example, a wristwatch device will provide accurate, ongoing information on your health status.

You will likely have powerful in-home expert systems, probably supplied by your health-care provider, which will not only aid diagnosis but also reinforce the pursuit of your chosen health goals. These expert systems, or electronic personal guides, will tailor the information to your knowledge level, interest level, and learning style, as well as those of your family members, each of whom would have a personal electronic 'health coach.' If you are genetically or otherwise inclined to heart disease, your coach will encourage specific preventive measures."[2]

The assumption here is that 50 percent of the variance of the causes of preventable premature death is due to behavior (20 percent is related to genes, 20 percent environment, and 10 percent medical care). It is this 50 percent that the health-bot—the health professional on a wrist—will help us manage. We can always take the devices off unless insurance companies require their continuous use for cheaper premiums.

Smarter consumers will undoubtedly check on medical research studies and be able to maneuver in a world of conflicting data and paradigms. This should make the job of general doctors easier. As smart cards and health-bots continue to evolve, their intelligence will probably reduce the frequency of, and need for, doctor visits, saving money spent on the health system.

Combined with the information and technology revolution, we may soon have the equivalent of hospitals on our wrists, actually, within our bodies. This should force general doctors to quickly become Internet-savvy, seeing it as a way to communicate with patients, especially younger patients raised on the Net—the "dot-com generation" now in the nation's high schools.

### GENETICS

Geneticists argue that genes play a role much larger than 20 percent in explaining our well-being, and genomics and germ-line engineering are expected to have an ever-greater impact on our health. The first step is identifying diseases to which we are predisposed. Next is customized gene therapy (replacing a defective gene and, therefore, a disease-causing gene with a healthy one). Further ahead is body-part cloning (growing replica parts to replace faulty ones).

The revolution's *full* potential lies with germ-line engineering, which modifies or manipulates the human DNA, for example, by altering the DNA of an unborn child to eliminate or decrease a predisposition toward a given disease. Germ-line engineering can also preselect ideal sperm and eggs for fertilization, thus affecting the germ lines of generations to come. At this stage, there appears to be few limits—with science fiction even too timid.

## PHARMACOGENOMICS

Pharmacogenomics entail examining inherited variations in genes that dictate drug response. Doctors can then explore ways these variations can be used to predict whether you will have a good response to a drug, a terrible one, or no response at all.

At present we can be given medications that either don't work or have bad side effects. Pharmacogenomics would make possible a day when your doctor would know you could suffer a severe negative reaction to a particular medication after a simple and rapid test of your DNA. Or your doctor would know you would greatly benefit from a new drug on the market, with little likelihood of a negative reaction. Proponents do not see this as a minor gain but part of a major renaissance in medical practice.

Note should be taken of the belief that while "the science of pharmacogenomics will provide an increased level of accuracy in selecting specific drug therapy for individual patients, it will not replace the art of clinical judgment in practice because of the confluence of social, behavioral, economic, and environmental factors."[3]

## NANOTECHNOLOGY

If nanotechnology delivers what it promises, our entire bodies will become a pharmaceutical factory, ready to detect, diagnose, and react to imbalances. Consider the claims of the Foresight Institute headed by Eric Drexler: "A mouthwash full of smart nanomachines could do all that brushing and flossing do and more, and with far less effort—making it more likely to be used. This mouthwash would identify and destroy pathogenic bacteria while allowing the harmless flora of the mouth to flourish in a healthy ecosystem."[4]

* Medical nanodevices could augment the immune system by finding and disabling unwanted bacteria and viruses.
* Medical nanodevices will be able to stimulate and guide the body's own construction and repair mechanisms to restore healthy tissue.
* Viruses can be eliminated by molecular-level cellular surgery. The required devices could be small enough to fit entirely within the cell, if need be.

In the United States, funding for nanotechnology has risen from $100 million in 1997 to $400 million in 2002; outside the United States, funding is approximately $1 billion. In November 2003, the U.S. Senate approved funding of $3.7 billion over four years for nanotech research.[5]

However, Professor Ken Donaldson of the University of Edinburgh warns: "Nanotechnology threatens to generate new hazards in the form of toxic molecules that can enter the lungs."[6] But the promises are dramatic.

In his book, *Nanomedicine*, Robert Freitas writes: "Once nanomachines are available, the ultimate dream of every healer, medicine man, and physician throughout recorded history will, at last, become a reality. Programmable and controllable microscale robots composed of nanoscale parts fabricated to nanometer precision will allow medical doctors to execute curative and reconstructive procedures in the human body at the cellular and molecular levels. Nanomedicine will employ molecular machine systems to address medical problems, and will use molecular knowledge to maintain and improve human health at the molecular scale ..."[7]

The Fred Hutchinson Cancer Research Center in Seattle is involved in a collaborative effort with Intel Corporation of Palo Alto, California, in which Intel will build a Raman Bioanalyzer System at the center, according to a press release.

"The instrument is normally used to detect microscopic imperfections in silicon chips. The cancer research center will beam the bioanalyzer's lasers onto medical samples, such as blood serum, to create images that reveal the chemical structure of molecules, helping to analyze, diagnose and prevent cancer."[8]

"This collaboration is a unique and exciting interaction," said Lee Hartwell, director of the center. "Biologists have never before had such a method for studying the molecular structure of biology. This is true discovery-based research; we don't know what we will see or learn."[9]

Mihail Roco, senior adviser for nanotechnology at the National Science Foundation in the United States, says the hope is to eliminate all cancers by 2015 using nanotechnology: "This is not a dream but a vision based on a well-defined strategy."[10]

Continues Freitas: "Nanomedical physicians of the early twenty-first century will still make good use of the body's natural healing powers and homeostatic mechanisms, because, all else equal, those interventions are best that intervene least. But the ability to direct events in a controlled fashion at the cellular level is the key that will unlock the indefinite extension of human health and the expansion of human abilities."[11]

**ALTERNATIVE MEDICINE**

By this I mean the move toward alternative or complementary medicine, primarily drawing on Chinese and Indian traditions of meditation and acupuncture but also less accepted alternatives like homeopathy (from Germany).

The data are stunning. In the United States, a Harvard Medical School study reports that 64 percent of medical schools now offer elective courses in complementary medicine. One in every three American adults uses chiropractic, acupuncture, and homeopathy treatments. Many patients judge conventional medicine as ineffectual, too costly, and/or too centered on curing ills rather than helping people maintain good health. These patients appreciate doctors who tend to spend greater amounts of time with them and who customize therapy. Also, scientific studies by Dr. Dean Ornish support diet, lifestyle, stress management, and social inclusion as factors to reverse heart disease.[12]

## AGING

While genomics, health-bots, and alternative therapies may make us healthier, the data generally do not look good for the aged. The average person is sick or disabled for nearly 80 percent of the extra years of life he or she gains as life expectancy rises. Health expenditures for those over age sixty-five are much higher than for the rest of the population. The World Health Organization estimates that by 2020 depression will be the leading cause of "disability adjusted life years," dramatically increasing the demands for psychiatric health services for young and old. The aged, particularly those removed from family and community, are especially prone to mental illnesses.[13]

## SUMMARY: CAREER CHOICES

What, then, might a would-be doctor want to consider now about the likely future for medicine?

1) Doctors will have to augment their understanding of the Internet, becoming knowledge navigators. However, they will also have to focus on what technology cannot give—warmth, human understanding, and empathy—as well as what some alternative therapies cannot give either—tough, rigorous analysis.

2) Health-bots and the Internet are likely to reduce the profits on the mass-market health business, especially since the patient-in, patient-out system appears not to be what users want.

3) If you are thinking about becoming a doctor, you will want to find specific niches not being met by a doctors.com-like Web site, the alternative medical care system, or genomics. Or you may want to focus on specific demographic groups and find out what their needs are—the global teenager, or the aged, who will need extra care.

Generally doctors will need to ask: What level of technology are they familiar with? Can they become knowledge navigators? Can they use the new technologies to increase their own quality of life; using the Net for seamless administration, so that their hours can be more flexible? Can they enter into dialogue with complementary medicine or at least begin to listen carefully to patients' concerns about their treatment? General doctors will have to reinvent themselves, detailing what role they desire for themselves in the future.

## NOTES

1  See www.metafuture.org for articles and books by Sohail Inayatullah.
2  See Clement Bezold, "Will Heart Disease Be Eliminated in Your Lifetime? The Best of Health Futures," *Futures Research Quarterly* (Summer 1995) and *The Future of Complementary and Alternative Approaches in U.S. Health Care*. Institute for Alternative Futures, 1998.
3  http://www.pharmaco-genomics.co.uk/contentpage.asp?contentid=19. Accessed 12 January 2004.
4  www.foresight.org/Utf/Unbound_LBW/chapt_10.html. Accessed 16 November 2003.
5  www.nanobusiness.org/pgepolicy.html. Accessed 18 December 2003.
6  www.smalltimes.com. "Researcher Warns of Toxic Threat from Nanotechnology." Accessed 19 November 2003.
7  www.foresight.org/Nanomedicine/Respirocytes.html. Accessed 16 November 2003.
8  http://www.intel.com/pressroom/archive/releases/20031023corp_a.htm. Accessed 28 October 2003.
9  Ibid.
10 www.smalltimes.com. Steve Mitchell, "Nanomedicine Vital to Finding a Cancer Cure," UPI. Accessed 1 November 2003.
11 www.foresight.org/Nanomedicine/Respirocytes.html. Accessed 16 November 2003.

12  Clement Bezold, "Health Care Faces a Dose of Change," *The Futurist*, April 1999, 30–33.
13  www.who.org. See World Health Organization, *The Global Burden of Disease*, 1996.

**DISCUSSION QUESTIONS+**

* How should current resources be invested: Research for the future or treatments for the present?

* What is the "right" balance of private sector vs. government investment in these new technologies?

* What should the government expect for its investments?

* Why will globalization undermine universal health care?

* How could globalization encourage universal health care?

* What is the difference between health information and knowledge?

* Why/how could health-bots "save" money?

* Could more information/knowledge lead to more health-care costs?

* What are the implications of more access to health information for general education?

* Could health literacy or the lack thereof become a challenge for these new technologies?

* What are the ethical/moral challenges to access to greater health information?

* Who is responsible/liable for information quality?

* Given that genotype is not phenotype, what are the ethical/moral implications of genetic manipulation? That is, are there risks associated with manipulating genes/germ cells because they have a propensity, not a certainty, for affecting health?

* Should genetic enhancements be subsidized or only used to care for illnesses?

* What are the implications for society, technology as a whole, health, and other areas if one of these technologies proves to be a disaster?

* The article focuses on individual health. What about public health considerations and these technologies?

+ *Prepared by Daniel Shostak, a health-care futurist, at the request of the editor.*

# IS THERE A UNION IN YOUR FUTURE?

David Reynolds, Ph.D.

Center for Labor Studies, Wayne State University

Have you worked after school, on weekends, and/or in the summers? If so, how much say did you have at work? Could you negotiate for a raise? If your supervisor was mean, could you get help? A *no* answer to any of these questions identifies you as part of the 87 percent of the workforce without the protection of a labor union (and a negotiated work contract, a formal grievance process, and a shop steward to speak up for you).

What might our country be like if, in the foreseeable future, not the current 13 percent, but the half or more of all workers who want to be in a union got their wish? What sort of difference might it make? Would a more unionized America be more or less to your liking?

## WHAT IS A UNION?

We have some sixty-three labor unions in the United States, each with hundreds of locals at several thousand work sites. Contrary to popular image, most members today do not work in factories. In fact, public school teachers form two of the nation's largest labor unions. Many doctors, lawyers, college professors, computer programmers, professional athletes, and even musicians and film stars are union members. Workers in a wide range of service jobs—like retail clerks, parking attendants, nursing aides, janitors, and security guards—are in unions.

The law defines a union as an organization of workers who have decided to work together for their own mutual aid and protection. They can sit down with their employer and negotiate the terms of their employment. They can talk about and seek to improve their wages, benefits, and conditions at work. Agreements between workers and the company are then written down into legally binding contracts.

Unions are democratic organizations. Members run for office and elect leaders. Members vote on important decisions like approving a contract or going on strike. Contrary to false images of constant confrontation between unions and management, once the issue of a union's existence has been settled, the vast majority of all contract negotiations end in mutual agreements without a strike.

### WHY UNIONS?

Employers are not elected yet they have all the power. You enjoy far less government protections at work than you probably realize. For one thing, the law allows your employer to fire you at any time—he/she does not need to give a reason. While laws try to protect you against racial, ethnic, and gender discrimination, and against unsafe working conditions, the government agencies responsible for enforcing these laws are chronically underfunded, understaffed, and hobbled by a schedule of very low fines and penalties.

Workers who join unions see themselves as gaining protections against authoritarian abuse and bringing democratic values into their workplace. A union contract provides workers the right to a fair hearing if they do not think the employer has treated them fairly. Union seniority systems provide workers greater job security the longer they stay at the company. Through unions, workers also push for educational benefits that help pay for a college education or life-long schooling. Across the country, grass-roots partnerships among unions, the community, and management promote "high-road" business practices of worker training, product quality, worker empowerment, and environmental responsibility.

To top it off, being a union member pays! In 2003, full-time workers who were union members earned on average $160 more per week than workers not in a union.[1] Also, union members generally enjoy better access to health care, pension, paid vacation, and other benefits. For example, while three-quarters of union members receive employer health insurance, only half of nonunion workers do.[2] Because workers can speak with a collective voice to enforce the laws, unionized workplaces tend to be cleaner, healthier, and safer. (With about eight thousand workers killed on the job each year, employees need a way to push for safe workplaces.)[3]

Nonunion employers often claim that the better wages and benefits workers gain through unions are too expensive. However, years of research have shown that companies also gain in the long run from being unionized. Such workplaces tend to have lower employee turnover and higher worker morale. A review of research, published in *Scientific America*, found that union workplaces are 16 percent more productive than nonunion workplaces.[4]

### HOW ARE UNIONS FARING?

On paper, workers have a legally protected right to organize a union. In reality, many employers vigorously oppose unionization. The government's enforcement of the legal right to unionize (granted by Congress in 1935) is so weak as to be meaningless. Every year, for example, more than twenty thousand workers are illegally fired by their employers simply because they spoke out in favor of unionization.[5] Unions have declined from representing about one-third of the workforce in 1953 to just less than 13 percent today.

Yet, according to the recent polls sponsored by organized labor, nearly half of the 110 million Americans who work in nonunion workplaces *would* form a union if given a fair and protected chance.[6] Were these 55 million people to join the ranks of 16 million union members, the labor movement would include a vast majority of working Americans.

Unions are stronger in most other industrialized countries. Nearly all workers in Sweden, Norway, and Denmark (including most managers) are in unions. The majority of

German workers are covered by union contracts. In Canada, one out of every three workers is a union member.[7]

## HOW UNIONS MIGHT TRANSFORM SOCIETY

Given this backdrop, what might a more unionized America look like? Unions have always had a big impact. U.S. workers won changes in the turbulent nineteenth century that at the time seemed like starry-eyed "utopian" dreams—an eight-hour workday (it had been twelve hours); a two-day weekend (it had been one: Sabbath Day); and bans on child labor (which had been widespread—and deadly). Comparing our country with more unionized societies of Canada and Europe points to how stronger unions might transform the United States.

The future of the standard of living of most people will be affected by whether more workers soon join unions. Historically, the average wages of people in and out of unions increased as unions grew. Similarly, as unions have become weaker, the buying power of the average wage-earner has fallen, and the gap between the rich and poor has increased.[8]

Early in the twentieth century, unions fought for and won the passage of minimum-wage laws as a public standard that prevents employers from driving wages too low. Over the last twenty years, however, the minimum wage has not kept pace with inflation. The current $5.15-an-hour federal minimum wage should be at least $9 an hour if workers are to live above the poverty line.[9] Recent campaigns by unions and their religious and community allies have raised the minimum wage in several states to $6.75 an hour.

Today almost half of all union members are women. Through unions, workers in female-dominated occupations would likely seek tough new regulations assuring that they receive wages fully equal to those in *comparable* male-dominated professions. Similarly, unions would support laws to require employers to provide part-time, temporary, and other contingent workers—many of whom are your high school buddies—the same wages and pro-rated benefits as their full-time employees. While generally people of color earn less than whites, this racial wage gap all but disappears in the unionized parts of our economy.

Just as workers fought for the forty-hour workweek decades ago, today workers use unions to gain more control over work time. With increased union political power, all workers might soon enjoy legally mandated paid vacations. In other more unionized countries, workers receive four to eight weeks off a year. Because of recent union contract bargaining and political action, many workers in Germany and everyone in France now have a thirty-five-hour workweek. In the 1990s, Denmark and Norway extended the idea of sabbatical leave—common among college faculty—to grant *every* citizen the right, once in their life, to take a year of *paid* leave from work to do whatever they want.

In the United States, unions lobbied in the early 1990s to pass the current legal right of workers to twelve weeks of unpaid leave from their jobs to care for a newborn infant or a fatally ill or enfeebled elderly relative. Today, they are advocating for paid leave. In Sweden, the labor movement won laws giving parents fifteen months of paid leave for each newborn child—the government picks up the person's salary.[10] Unions in many countries have also pushed for the right of parents to take time off work to participate in their child's school activities.

In the nineteenth century, unions fought for the basic right of children—irrespective of their families' ability to pay—to go to school. Our free public-school system is the result. In Europe, union political action pushed for free university education, with the government providing stipends to cover room and board. Teens who choose not go to college often typically enroll in some form of comprehensive high-quality job-training system run jointly by unions and companies. The state certifies these vocational skills so that workers can go to any employer with a record of proven competence.

More union strength today could lead to other forms of public wealth. For example, the United States is the only industrialized country not to have some form of national public health care covering everyone. Thanks to union political action, people in Canada and Europe simply walk into a medical facility or doctor's office and have their health needs met. Just like our schools, this sort of health system is paid for through taxes.

Unions traditionally have pushed for progressive tax systems in which people and companies contribute based on their true ability to pay. In many parts of Europe, people retire fully on public pensions that often count time spent in education or raising children as work for pension credits.

### DEMOCRACY EVERYWHERE

Since they are organizations of ordinary people, unions around the world are at the forefront of democratic struggles. Indeed, one of the first things dictators, like Adolf Hitler or Saddam Hussein, do when they seize power is to outlaw authentic unions. In our country, more than a century and a half ago unions fought for and won the right for working people to vote (originally you could only vote if you owned enough property).

In the United States today, unions have joined with community groups to call for election campaign finance reform. Candidates for state and national office have to raise millions of private dollars and most of this money comes from the wealthiest few percent of Americans. For every dollar that unions raise for elections, for example, corporations give from $11 to $20.[11] By contrast, in countries with strong labor movements, elections are financed with public funds so that candidates are not beholden to private contributors. In Europe, usually one of a country's two or three main political parties was built by workers through their labor movements.

Because of strong unions, German workers at large firms enjoy the democratic right to elect half of their company's supervisory board. And in every workplace, employees can elect Works Councils with the legal authority to participate in day-to-day decisions.[12] Involving more voices in company decisions has been a central part of Germany's economic success and a continuing goal of unions in Europe and our country.

### THE FUTURE IS BEING MADE TODAY

In 1995, the new leadership of the AFL-CIO—the national

umbrella organization to which most American unions belong—was facing an uncertain future. Over the last half-century, unions had declined from representing one-third to less than one out of seven workers. While nonunion employers are increasingly hostile to unions and the legal protections for workers are increasingly weak, AFL-CIO leaders have also realized that unions have not tried to organize vast numbers of new members in a long time.

In response, the AFL-CIO has called on unions to reach out to the 55 million Americans who are not in a union but want to be. And students are helping. Through the AFL-CIO's Union Summer program, for example, hundreds of high school and college students work every summer in paid internships helping workers to organize.

Unions are also returning to their roots as leaders of broad social change. For example, thanks to the efforts of labor-community coalitions, states like Vermont, Washington, Massachusetts, California, and Oregon have raised their minimum wage above federal standards in recent years. In more than 150 communities across the country, grass-roots living wage campaigns have won or are organizing for laws requiring companies that receive public contracts or financial assistance to pay wages above the poverty level.

In Maine, California, and other states, unions and community allies have lobbied for reforms to provide health insurance for all and to lower the costs of prescription drugs. With union support, voters in Maine, Massachusetts, and Arizona have set up clean election laws that allow candidates to run with public, rather than private money.

As the labor movement struggles to rebuild itself, it will increasingly join arms with emerging citizen movements to help transform the United States. Union organizing has always been a matter of social as well as economic gains—of raising moral standards, protecting civil rights, boosting community health, and promoting basic democracy.

NOTES

1   Union wage numbers in 2003:
    www.bls.gov/news.release/union2.nr0.htm.
2   "The Union Difference" in *America@Work*, August 2003.
3   www.semcosh.org/rory_oniell.htm.
4   Paul Wallich, "Look for the Union Label," *Scientific America*,
    August 1998.
5   Charles Morris, "A Tale of Two Statutes: Discrimination for
    Union Activity under the NLRA and RLA," *Employee Rights and
    Employment Journal*, vol. 2: 317, 322.
6   According to a poll conducted in 2002 by Peter D. Hart,
    48 percent of the 110 million U.S. workers who are not in a
    union would like to be in one.
7   Figures from Statistics Canada, U.S. Bureau of National Affairs,
    European Industrial Relations Observatory.
8   Chuck Collins and Felice Yeskel, *Economic Apartheid in America*:
    *A Primer on Economic Inequality and Security* (New York: The
    New Press, 2000).
9   In 2002, the federal poverty threshold for a family of four was
    $18,100. See http://aspe.hhs.gov/poverty/.
10  Gunilla Furst, *Sweden—The Equal Way* (Stockholm: The
    Swedish Institute, 2000).
11  For the latest information on who funds what candidates,
    including representatives in Congress, go to the Center for
    Responsible Politics at www.opensecrets.org.
12  David Reynolds, *Taking the High Road: Communities Organize for
    Economic Change*, chpt. 2 (Armonk, N.Y.: M.E. Sharpe, 2002).

FURTHER READING

Clawson, Dan. *The Next Upsurge: Labor and the New Social Movements.*
    Ithaca, N.Y.: Cornell University Press, 2003. Looks at how unions
    are linking up with civil rights groups, students, women's groups,
    environmentalists, and others.
Collins, Chuck, and Felice Yeskel. *Economic Apartheid in America.*

New York: The New Press, 2000. Covers the growing inequality in the United States and the grass-roots efforts to change it.

Freeman, Richard. *Working under Different Rules*. New York: Russell Safe Foundation, 1994. Summarizes the findings of a large-scale multi-year research project involving dozens of researchers.

Reynolds, David. *Taking the High Road: Communities Organize for Economic Change*. Armonk, N.Y.: M.E. Sharpe, 2002. Labor in Europe and labor-community activism today.

## Journals

*America@Work*—the AFL-CIO's monthly magazine.

*Working USA* and *New Labor Forum*—bring academics and activists together to discuss the future of the labor movement.

*Labor Notes*—covers today's unions from the perspective of many dissident groups within unions.

## WEB SITES

www.aflcio.org

The national union umbrella federation.

www.labornet.org

Great starting place with tons of information about unions.

www.uniondemocracy.com

Association for Union Democracy helps union members ensure that their union lives up to its democratic ideals.

www.workingforamerica.org

Union-business partnerships.

www.acorn.org

Organization of low-income people that is a prominent union ally.

www.walmartwatch.com

Example of a union campaign against a powerful and ugly employer.

www.asje.org

Alliance for Sustainable Jobs and the Environment, an example of how unions and environmentalists can cooperate.

www.atwork.org

Model labor-community action in Silicon Valley.

www.laane.org

Model labor-community action in Los Angeles.

www.sweden.se

Information on Sweden, the most unionized country in the world.

www.publicampaign.org

Information on campaign finance reform.

Courtesy of The Venus Project
Designed by Jacque Fresco and Roxanne Meadows

# Part Two

## CHALLENGED AT HOME

*If global problems seem too large*
*for most people to grapple with,*
*it is within our reach to take*
*responsibility for our home places.*
—Freeman House,
"A Watershed Runs through You."

Four essays in this section speak to challenges close to us. The first essay explores what K–12 schooling might resemble if and when we finally decide to make a warranted investment in computer power access. The second essay asks a similar question, this time about our investing in rehabilitation for criminal offenders, the better to upgrade life in a future "we will undoubtedly share with tomorrow's criminals." The third essay looks back from 2051, and highlights several attractive developments we could promote between now and then, not the least of which is a novel way of mitigating the worst aspects of uneven income distribution. The closing essay shares a dream of having many cities at sea (literally, each occupying its own ocean-going vessel). This would enable a large-scale real-time experiment in offering varied lifestyles to all takers. Many readers, I suspect, will wish they might soon come aboard.
—Editor

# SCHOOLING IN 2010: HELPING YOUNG LEARNERS SOAR!

Arthur B. Shostak, Ph.D.

Emeritus Professor of Sociology, Drexel University

By 2010, more extraordinary and desirable changes could occur in K–12 schooling than in the previous fifty years! If parents insist that local school boards and the states do the right thing, the schooling of our children, whether public or private, could be very much better, and far different than anything you and I can recall, thereby scaring as well as thrilling us.

Consider the radical changes in education made possible by "Buck Rogers" advances in computer applications. To educate is to first communicate, and the gadgets coming our way are remarkably powerful communication aids. Electronic books as portable libraries, computers as "wearables," information agents as allies, and virtual reality labs as "way out" simulations, offer much, especially as they achieve simplicity, versatility, and pleasurability. Whether we will take full advantage of their potential, however, remains uncertain.

By 2010, many teachers and youngsters could be savvy users of remarkable computer-aided electronic books. They would enable a child to carry around an entire bookshelf programmed into one lightweight attractive volume (and easily repro-grammed as the teacher and/or the child wishes). Each could have a built-in dictionary, a thesaurus, word-search capability, excellent screen resolution, and a long battery life. Each would enable a child to rewrite the story itself, such as by putting himself or herself into the tale. An embedded voice chip would help tutor the child eager to learn how to read better and could provide immediate self-scoring quizzes with which to assure a youngster he or she was really "getting it."

By 2010, many teachers and youngsters could also be savvy users of very powerful wireless computers carried on their person. Known as "wearables," they might take the form of a Palmtop (a mini-laptop) or a watch-like gadget worn on the wrist. Users would speak to, and be spoken to by "wearables," whose small size belies their very great significance.

Imagine your child able to learn almost anything he or she is curious about, whenever they want, wherever they might be, and in such a way as to bolster the youngster's self-esteem, natural curiosity, and love of learning. Imagine your child able to do this alone or with others; in small doses or for hours on end; in the company of brothers or sisters, or in immediate touch with youngsters from around the world. Imagine all of this in synch with the values of your family and free of hazards otherwise posed by unfriendly cyberspace material. Neat, yes?! And, thanks to "wearables" previewed in 1999, they are highly likely to characterize schooling in 2010.

When a large, heavy, and awkward computer is no longer left behind on the desk, or lugged about as a six-pound bulky laptop but is instead a very convenient small wireless aid, schoolchildren will be empowered as never before. A child can whisper any question posed by a teacher into his or her "wearable." An Information Broker hovering nearby in cyberspace will be eager to sell information from vast data banks for a trivial sum. The broker will "sell" the youngster a good answer in nano- or pico-seconds. This sort of regurgitation of facts, an outmoded form of miseducation, should give way to far more creative mind-stretching challenges.

Housed in a child's "wearable" is likely to be a twenty-first century version of Merlin, Puff the Magic Dragon, Jiminy Cricket, Tinker Bell, Aristotle, and many of the other magical "aha!" aides of which a child might dream. Known technically as an Intelligent Agent, it amounts to artificial intelligence software programmed to do its creator's bidding.

A child would essentially "train" his or her Agent by patiently answering its endless stream of ever-more-refined questions (for example, What are your favorite toys? Why? Least favorite? Why?). In this way, the Agent would get to "know" the youngster (whose well-being would be at the heart of the software's "existence"). Much like a Furby, the 1998 Christmas gift sensation, the child's Intelligent Agent would get "smarter" with use, grow on (and with) one, and occasionally surprise and delight its young caretaker.

Any question that might occur to a child could be asked of its Intelligent Agent, which, in turn, would rapidly research the matter in cyberspace, using search engines vastly improved over those crude upstarts familiar in 2005 (Yahoo, AltaVista, etc.). In school, a child's Agent would stand by ready to provide whatever information its young "creator" might need.

As if this were not enough, a child might "train" his or her Agent to provide counsel, solace, support, advice, or just plain friendly chit-chat, much as every child occasionally wants. At home, the Agent could offer a shoulder to cry or lean on, provide a wise head with which to argue, and in 1,001 other ways, be a nonjudgmental, unflappable, and thoroughly reliable pal.

As if electronic books, computers as "wearables," and Intelligent Agents were not enough, K–12 schooling in 2010 could also use the most exotic learning tool of all, virtual reality aids to education. As long ago as the mid-1990s, especially adventurous school districts created virtual reality labs in which youngsters could don goggles, take a joystick in hand, and "magically" transport themselves via VR computer simulations inside of molecules, algebraic formulas, or oceans they wanted to study. These "wrap-around environments" enabled children, as telepresences, to "drop in" on VR recreations of the signing of the Constitution, Dr. Martin Luther King's seminal address at the Civil Rights March, or the impeachment of President Andrew Johnson.

A dramatic complement to the four-thousand-year-old conventional classroom system, virtual reality programs enable youngsters to "feel" like they were "there," interact with other participants, and explore what it would mean to modify the (artificial) world itself.

Virtual reality breaks down the traditional and costly distinction among work, play, and education. It offers the possibility of a class choosing to "meet" in a simulation of Antarctica, Brazil, Croatia, Denmark, or Ghana. It allows participants to explore the enormity of our solar system by "moving" around in it, or to get inside the microworld of bacteria. Best of all, virtual reality essentially dissolves the wall of the schoolhouse and offers educational access to the universe.

Naturally, to host such advances, K–12 classrooms should house phone lines, cutting-edge modems, and/or infrared equipment designed to help a youngster move with his or her "wearable" (and Intelligent Agent) effortlessly from room to room. Teachers could rely on timely material drawn immediately from the Web and made available on the screen of every child's "wearable." Learners would be able to input ideas into everyone else's "wearable," thereby elevating educational dialogue ("interactivity") to a new plane. Ideas should crackle around high-tech-aided classrooms, now finally as vital and as engaging as playtime is in the schoolyard.

Lest the impression be left that educational technology alone is all that could and should improve by 2010, it is also critical to note the urgent need between now and then to reduce the size of classes, employ more new findings about learning, raise the pay of the staff, emphasize the arts, upgrade standards—and spend the vast amounts necessary to "walk the talk."

By 2010, no subject is likely to prove as central as the arts, for they stand out in their ability to celebrate our human distinctiveness. Youngsters are likely to inherit a world where "smart" equipment, exemplified by the Intelligent Agents in their "wearables," takes the place of humans in doing rote, repetitive, programmable tasks (those that require precision and are hugely intolerant of error). The jobs left to human job seekers will require creativity, ingenuity, inventiveness, resourcefulness, and even zaniness, fantasy, and fun. The arts uniquely help youngsters nurture their natural gifts in these domains and learn to accommodate the messy, imprecise ways of their fellows. Playfulness will prosper as never before in K–12 schooling.

Which is not the same thing as saying content loses. Quite the contrary. Standards will be more critical than ever: In order to graduate from high school in 2010, all teens (not just college-bound youngsters) could be required to pass no-nonsense statewide exams in American history, English, global studies, math, and science (as in New York State since 1999). All may be required to try out career options via co-op stints and also satisfy a community-service requirement. As well, high school graduates could come with a "money-back" guarantee—if he or she cannot do the job, they can be "returned" by a supportive employer for additional free remedial schooling (as in Los Angeles since 1997).

Similarly, before new teachers can be hired, they could have to pass several difficult tests and get a license from a thirty-five-state consortium that began in 2003. Special attention should be paid to their "usability" craft, their ability to make sound and creative use of high-tech educational tools. Accountability could be crisply measured, merit pay could be a significant portion of total compensation, and teachers' unions could be at the forefront of the reform effort, as so often in the past.

By this time you have undoubtedly noticed the use over and again of the word "could." There are no guarantees in any of this. Many previous waves of technological innovation have disappointed. Classroom use of television in the 1980s was supposed to make the difference, as was computer-assisted instruction in the 1990s but both appear mixed blessings. Similarly, only one child in four is presently being offered any arts education (music, arts, theater) at least once a week in school.

Nothing—not educational technology gains, staff aids, curriculum changes, and/or increased standards—are sure things. The only sure thing is that achieving any of these digital-based reforms by 2010 will require many hard-to-raise tax dollars.

Why, then, are they still good bets? Because the alternative guarantees local and national disaster. Governors know that jobs and new businesses early in the twenty-first century will go only to states with a top-notch entry-level workforce. They understand how fierce the competition is among states for educational bragging rights ("the best schools in the East"). Either we invest substantially in K–12 possibilities, or we will fall further behind forty-nine other state competitors, watch our best graduates increasingly pack up for better jobs elsewhere, and wanly rue our shortsighted mistake.

Between now and 2010, we have to close the educational gap between Information Have-More and Information Have-Less neighbors. As economist Lester C. Thurow explains, the contest in the world is not between the top 20 percent of every nation but between the rest of every nation's workforce. Unless and until the vast number of Americans get out of the Have-Less category, none of us will have the security and well-being we want for all. Not until every child has the advantages characteristic today only of affluent school districts and high-profile private schools will our position in the global economic competition be secure.

If we elect to shortchange our offspring and nickel-and-dime our educational efforts, not even our Intelligent Agents in 2010 can keep us from social and economic disaster. But in a bold new world of ubiquitous computing, with the help of such Agents, of versatile electronic books, computers as "wearables," exotic virtual reality labs, and other "Buck Rogers" educational aids, we may yet achieve an educational system as delightful and rewarding as our children (and their caring teachers, administrators, and building staff) have always deserved.

FURTHER READING

**Articles**

Buchen, Irving H. "Education in America: The Next Twenty-Five Years." *The Futurist*, January–February 2003, 44–50. Outlines "some of the most likely essential features of education of 2025."

Riel, Margaret. "The Future of the Classroom ... : New Modes of Teaching and Learning." In *Catalog of Tomorrow: Trends Shaping Your Future*, edited by Andrew Zolli. Indianapolis, Ind.: 2003, 192–193. Details a glowing vision of schooling in 2015 and makes a case for the indispensability of rapid change in its direction.

## Books

Boyer, William H. *Education for the Twenty-First Century*. San Francisco, Calif.: Caddo Gap Press, 2002. Contends that schools should help create the future by intent, be problem-centered, emphasize participation in social change, encourage group processes, and study alternative futures.

Fullan, Michael. *Change Forces with a Vengeance*. New York: Routledge/Falmer, 2003. Provides eight guidelines/lessons for large-scale reform of schooling, with an emphasis on moral purpose, quality relationships, and quality ideas.

Hicks, David. *Lessons for the Future: The Missing Dimension in Education*. New York: Routledge/Falmer, 2002. Makes a strong case for futures material in the schooling of students of all ages. Offers pragmatic advice on how to include futuristic methods in the classroom, and how to persuade schools and parents of the need for the same.

St. John, Edward P. *Refinancing the College Dream: Access, Equal Opportunity, and Justice for Taxpayers*. Baltimore, Md.: Johns Hopkins University Press, 2003. Explains that the recent shift in the burden of paying for college from the government to the student erodes equal opportunity for low-income young adults. Proposes reforms, since the distribution of the opportunity to attend college "is fundamental to liberty and social justice."

Thernstrom, Abigail and Stephan. *No Excuses: Closing the Racial Gap in Learning*. New York: Simon & Schuster, 2003. Argues that "the central civil rights issue of our time is our failure to provide first-class education for black and Hispanic students, in both cities and suburbs." Supports the availability of charter schools and vouchers.

Toch, Thomas. *High Schools on a Human Scale: How Small Schools Can Transform American Education*. Boston, Mass.: Beacon Press, 2003. Details five stories of successful small high schools (less than four hundred students), each with a defining characteristic of high academic expectations for every student.

### Newspapers/Magazines

*ESchool News: Technology News for Today's K–20 Educator* (www.eschool-news.org). Outstanding coverage of the ways to use technology and the Internet to transform schools and achieve high educational goals.

*Technology & Learning* (www.techlearning.com)
Monthly coverage of the ways K–12 educators can better manage, teach, and train with technology.

# ALTERNATIVE FUTURES OF CRIME AND PRISONS

## Sohail Inayatullah, Ph.D.

Editor, *Journal of Futures Studies*

One way to understand the future of crime and corrections is through popular movies. In *Logan's Run*, for example, living past thirty was in effect a crime. As we rapidly age throughout the world, we can see that criminal activity of the aging will become an issue. The definitions and the means of crime traditionally associated with males ages fifteen to twenty-five are likely to change with an aging society.

In *Blade Runner*, the criminals were replicants—biogenetically engineered individuals who performed the tasks humans did not desire to do. They were banned from Earth, and if they secretly returned, they were hunted down and "retired" (turned off permanently) by "Blade Runners" (police specialists). Crime thus was associated with the undesirability of coexisting with a new species (one that we created). As the science and technology revolution continues to explode, wildly new crimes associated with out-of-control robots and vicious computer viruses are certainly likely to increase and grow, becoming far more serious threats than they are today.

Not only are the dangers riskier, but the science and technology revolution is providing new tools to address crime. For example, new forms of lie detection, based not on anxiety but on brain scanning, are likely to enhance the probability of apprehending criminals. The movie *Minority Report* takes this much further with psychics somehow gaining the ability to predict crime. Police appear at a crime scene just *before* the criminal act is actually committed. However, and not surprisingly, mistakes are made. Eventually the program must be abandoned but not before considerable harm is done. Increasingly, we can expect varied attempts to intervene earlier in the crime cycle.

Postmodernists, such as the philosopher Michel Foucault, help us focus with fresh eyes on the definition of crime. For example, imagine a future society where because of water scarcity, watering your lawn becomes a crime. Who are the likely prison-goers then? Or imagine a future vegetarian society where those who eat meat are sent to prison. What would our prisons look like then? What would be an appropriate sentence for a meat eater? What would early intervention be like? Virtual reality movies of chickens being killed? A weekly assortment of the best vegetarian food?

Thus, to understand the future of prisons and the future of crime we need to understand the nature of society: What is most important? What do we value today? What will we value tomorrow?

### AT ISSUE: REHABILITATION?

In the United States and most developed nations, the main debate involves rehabilitation versus punishment. Those on the rehabilitation side believe crimes are generally committed for social and economic reasons.

You undoubtedly know the argument: Born into a poor family, or a single-parent family, a person goes to a second-rate public school that labels him or her an underachiever. Over time, the person sees him or herself as not very worthwhile. Eventually, noticing the relative deprivation—that others are driving fancier cars, have more "perfect" wives and girlfriends, live in beautiful estates—the person steals or commits other crimes.

Imprisoning someone like that is thought to merely add to the problem. In jail, offenders rarely learn new skills, except criminal ones. Their peer group consists of other prisoners, with similar stories. When they are released from prison, they stay within their learned behavior and thus are likely to commit more crimes.

If you believe in this perspective, the reform interventions needed are multifold:

1) Remove class barriers. Ensure that the possibility to move from the lower to the middle class and even to the upper class is there for all. Society should be based on merit.

2) Help single-parent families. By ensuring that children of single-parent families do not fall into the poverty trap, the chances of future crimes are reduced. Funding can come through various programs. Ensuring breakfast for children, housing allowances, unemployment insurance, counseling, or any intervention that helps those outside of the system receive benefits that others are getting increases the possibility of people feeling they are part of society.

3) Promote finer peer groups. As children grow and develop their own peer groups, intervention comes through job training, sports camps, community clubs—again anything to ensure that children do not start on the path to crime; that they remain integrated in the community.

4) Create learning and healing communities. Ultimately, intervention is about healing communities, reweaving the fabric of friendship, and helping peers see that we are all in this together.

5) Rehabilitate through transforming the prison. The rehabilitation model in prisons also works to ensure that when a prisoner is released he will leave behind his previous behavior and start anew. Interventions range from changing diet (research suggests that diets rich in fruits and vegetables and low in refined sugar reduce prison violence), and changing the colors of prison cells, to giving prisoners meaningful work, having prison gardens (so inmates can connect with nature), and work training.

6) Use alternative sentencing. As much as possible, and where appropriate, keep those who have committed crimes out of prisons. Whether through electronic

sentencing, halfway houses, or volunteering, ensure that those sentenced find ways to reconnect, to psychologically earn their way back into society. European nations are especially having success with this approach.

The goal of this model is to ensure that the prisoner (and the victim and community) is healed; that connections among self, nature, God, and community are remade and restored. Once accomplished, the chances of the prisoner committing another offense are diminished. The scientific evidence is that this model *does* work.

### AT ISSUE: PUNISHMENT?

A second model argues that the first one gives the prisoner all the rights. And the victim—who may have been raped or maimed—has none. In this model, the best way to reduce present-day and future crimes is to keep serious offenders in jail. And there is evidence that backs this up—25 percent of criminal activity can be reduced by lengthy prison sentences.

Underneath this approach is the view that we should be punished if we do something wrong. We have sinned, whether against our community, ourselves, or our understanding of God. Merely focusing on rehabilitation sends a signal of weakness to potential criminals. The most extreme version of this is the death penalty. While most Western nations have eliminated it—seeing it as repugnant murder grievously committed by the state—the United States continues this ancient practice, as do most traditional feudal nations (some of which would stone an adulterous woman to death, a sentence generally protested by other nations, including the United States).

The punishment model also supports the war on drugs; the transformation of the prison through new surveillance technologies (making it safer for guards); restorative justice for victims; and privatizing prisons, to make them more efficient and cost-effective.

## NEW VARIABLES: GENETICS

The debate between rehabilitation and punishment is being challenged on multiple fronts. The genetics revolution, for one, is searching for the roots of crime in our DNA. If certain individuals are more inclined toward committing crimes—as by their risk-taking proclivities—we should intervene to ensure that they do not behave this way. This means mapping our genes and our theories of the factors of crime. Intervention could take the form of gene therapy (healing the damaged gene array) or germ-line intervention (ensuring the faulty gene is eliminated so that future generations do not inherit the fault). These solutions can be accomplished at various phases in the "chain" of crime, even afterward. (In rape cases, judges have sentenced individuals to take castration drugs.)

## NEW VARIABLES: HARD AND SOFT TECH

Digitalization is important largely to prevent current and future crimes. With increased video surveillance, poorly lighted areas can be made safer. Child-nabbing is far less likely since surveillance cameras will be able to capture a picture of the abductor. Over time, bio-digital devices linked to global positioning systems (GPS) can be fitted on most humans so that the capacity to prevent crimes is dramatically increased. Bio-devices are already being used in electronic sentencing. For crimes that do not hurt others—like many drug crimes—home sentencing is gaining in use.

Over time, certain parts of a city could be seen as digital no-gos. A pedophile could be implanted with a device that warns the local prison/police center that he is nearing a primary school. In this sense, the new technologies allow us to place the prisoner in a limited exile. Instead of being sent far away, his capacity to move is limited. This enhances his chances of being rehabilitated as well as his chances of not offending again. Of course, many fear that with these "all-seeing eyes" the state could become too powerful, not only intervening in crime but intervening in private noncriminal behavior.

A relevant example of soft tech is India, which has found that prison violence is reduced and offenders are rehabilitated far more effectively if meditation is used as an intervention method. Prisoners find themselves calming down and having increased clarity on their present and futures.

## ALTERNATIVE FUTURES

We can usefully draw now on four radically different scenarios for the near-future:

1) Prisons Forever: A Continued Growth scenario forecasts still more prisons, more overcrowding, more law and order, with only minor and occasional swings to rehabilitation. Generally the focus is on the victim, crime prevention through increased policing, and incarceration. This scenario is both low tech and low community. The end result is probably increased crime, as offenders are not effectively rehabilitated. (Only 25 percent of the variation of crime can be explained by increased incarceration.)

   The drivers here are the law and order paradigm, punishment, the needs of the prison-industrial complex, the media, politicians, and political rhetoric.

2) Prisons Transformed: A second scenario focuses on achieving better outcomes within prisons through better prison design, cognitive therapy, health and human rights needs of prisoners, education, and other positive intervention.

   The drivers here include overcrowding in prisons, violence in prisons, the costs of prisons, globalization of human rights and human rights organizations, and the "what works" prison policy approach.

3) Community Alternatives: A third scenario focuses on community alternatives, including restorative justice and community building. Electronic monitoring and other high technologies allow increased mobility. Community reintegration is common. Surveillance comes from neighborhood residents and new

technologies. A small percentage of highly violent offenders still ends up in prisons.

The drivers here include the impact of pro-rehabilitation criminologists; the professional ideology of "what works"; the search for "community" in an increasingly fragmented world; cost savings; demographic changes; and new technologies.

4) Prevention: A fourth scenario ensures that societal conditions are changed so that individuals must rarely go to prison. Prevention has numerous dimensions, such as keeping families together; counseling for abused adolescents; better policing and surveillance (reducing the opportunities of crime); transforming prisons to bioscience intervention through identifying high-risk individuals; and creating a more equitable society.

The drivers here include a swing away from punishment, evidence-based criminology, a social welfare state, the human genome project, and other scientific breakthroughs in the life sciences.

Of these scenarios, which one do you think is most likely? Why? Most desirable? Why?

## NOVEL ALTERNATIVES

What of "Punishment Plus?" A correctional system that has elements of punishment but also strong elements of rehabilitation. In this unusual system, instead of being swayed by politicians, scientific policy studies would inform prison design and correctional policies. Thus, along with the prison, the system focuses on cognitive skills and a rehabilitative behavioral program. It would be restorative and yet also preventative.

One could also imagine a high-tech correctional system, perhaps run by a Corrections.com-type Web site. It would be a smart, adaptive, learning organization, working to not only ensure that crime was prevented (working with the police, counseling agencies) but also restoring community. In this future, the challenge would be to ensure that humane and ethical innovation was central to prisons and policing, instead of tolerating a laggard institution stuck in the medieval and industrial era.

## SUMMARY

Crime and corrections are based on our deep-held, unconscious view of criminality. While science and technology, hard and soft, race ahead, many penal institutions remain lost in time. The ideas that govern them remain based on traditional notions of crime and punishment (sin and hell) and traditional notions of imprisonment (the prison, the cell, the jailer, the watchful eye).

If we wish to transform these places, we need to ask what is our *preferred* view of crime and corrections? Which scenario do you prefer? What would be the most serious crimes? Less serious? Would you still have prisons? If so, how would they be designed?

Seen this way, the future of crime and corrections is less about forecasting new technologies, demographic shifts, or social movements, and more about asking *what type of world do we really want to live in?* And, what steps can we initiate *today* to help create that world?

## REFERENCES

Allard, Jacinthe, Carole Dolan and Pierre Cremer (eds.). *Reflections of a Canadian Prison Warden: The Visionary Legacy of Ron Wiebe: An Unfinished Conversation*. Correctional Service of Canada, 2000. http://www.csc-scc.gc.ca/text/pblct/ronweibe/3_e.shtml. Accessed 10 May 2002.

Atlas, Randall, Ph.D., AIA. *Changes in Prison Facilities as a Function of Correctional Philosophy*. Atlas Safety & Security Design, Inc. Miami, Fla.: www.cpted-security.com/prisons5.htm. Accessed 23 May 2002.

Blumstein, Alfred, and Joel Wallman. *The Crime Drop in America*. New York: Cambridge University Press, October 2000.

Abstracted by Michael Marien, *Future Survey* 22:12/584, December 2000.

Coyle, Andrew. *The Restorative Prison Project. The Myth of Prison Work.* Kings College London International Centre for Prison Studies, May 2001. http://www.kcl.ac.uk/depsta/rel/icps/worldbrief/world_brief.html. Accessed 17 May 2002.

Cullen, Francis T., and Paul Gendreau. "From Nothing Works to What Works. Changing Professional Ideology in the Twenty-First Century." *The Prison Journal.* Vol. 81, No. 3, 2001, 313–338.

Dator, James. www.futures.hawaii.edu/dator/courts/crimedontpay.html.

Foucault, Michel. *Discipline and Punish: The Birth of the Prison.* New York: Vintage Books, 1979.

www.gyre.org/news/related/Neurotechnology/Lie+Detector+Technology.

Inayatullah, Sohail. "Futures Research in the Hawaii Judiciary: An Overview." *World Future Society Bulletin.* Vol. 17, No. 6, 1983.

———, and Jennifer Fitzgerald. "Gene Discourses: Law, Politics, Culture, Future." *Journal of Technological Forecasting and Social Change.* Vol. 52, No. 2–3, June–July 1996, 161–183.

———. "The Rights of Robot: Inclusion, Courts and Unexpected Futures," *Journal of Futures Studies.* Vol. 6, No. 2, November 2001, 93–102.

"New Report Links Crime with Poverty." *Honolulu Advertiser,* 5 December 1999, A16.

Newell, Tim. "Responding to the Crisis, Belgium Establishes Restorative Prisons." International Centre for Prison Studies. http://www.kcl.ac.uk/depsta/rel/icps/worldbrief/world_brief.html. Accessed 16 April 2002.

"Punishment in the Netherlands." Willem Pompe Institute for Criminal Law and Criminology, Utrecht University, December 1996. http://www.ministerievanjustitie.nl:8080/B_ORGAN/wodc/summaries/ob164sum.htm. Accessed 9 May 2002.

Sneed, Catherine. "Seeds of Change." *Yes,* Fall 2000.

Stephens, Gene. "Preventing Crime: The Promising Road Ahead." *The Futurist,* 33:9, November 1999, 29–34. Abstracted by Michael Marien, *Future Survey* 22:2/07, 4 February 2000.

APPENDIX

Yogic masters like P.R. Sarkar argue that there are four reasons for crime: 1) snap judgment—based on a single emotional event; 2) hormonal reasons—an imbalanced body-mind system; 3) genetic; and 4) social and economic structures. For the first and second causes, he recommends yoga, meditation, and dietary change—soft sciences. For the third, prison is often best (but with the goal to rehabilitate), and for the fourth, social and community intervention (economic opportunities, responsibility setting, peer pressure). See: Sohail Inayatullah, *Understanding Sarkar*. Leiden, Netherlands: Brill, 2002.

For information on meditation in prisons, see: www.dhamma.org/prisons.htm and http://www.kiranbedi.com/vipasanainprisons.htm.

Crime and punishment is also based on the type of society one lives in. In a warrior-dominated society, where issues of loyalty, honor, and courage are foremost, punishment can be trying indeed. In warrior societies, like Saudi Arabia or Afghanistan, hands are cut off for certain offenses. In modern societies, where bureaucratic rules are foremost, the process of law has become most important. While we can never know for sure if someone committed a crime, we do our best to ensure that the process of justice is fair. Thus, the rights of a possible criminal are read. To those who cannot afford an attorney, the state provides a lawyer. A person is judged by a group of peers. The reasoning here is that it is far worse to punish an innocent person than to let the guilty go.

■ **Essay Eight** ■

# JANUARY 2051: A LETTER
# TO MY BEST BUD IN BANGLADESH

### Linda Brown
Futures/Market Researcher

*A vitiated state of morals, a corrupted public conscience,*
*is incompatible with freedom.*
—Patrick Henry

**INTRODUCTION**

I was first introduced to the idea of studying the future when I was in high school. It was a very short but vivid introduction. The reel-to-reel projector had just started clacking away, illuminating the white wall screen with a picture of someone with funky-colored, spiked hair. Was it purple or blue? It was something we had never seen before.

Suddenly, the principal burst into the classroom and forcibly ripped the tape off the projector. Apparently, discussing the future was too controversial then.

Since I never did see the rest of the movie, I cannot tell you if there was anything truly offensive in it or not. I can tell you I have since seen many people with funky-colored and spiked hair. I also want to tell Barbara Shelar, my high school teacher, "Thank you for introducing me to the idea of studying the future."

Have you ever seen anyone with hair dyed an unusual color or spiked? Have you ever seen a clackity reel-to-reel movie projector? Keep that in mind, when answering the survey at the end of this essay.

Written as a letter between teen pen pals in the world of 2051, this scenario challenges the reader with ideas of new political boundaries, an environmentally based global tax system, stagnation in the progress of women, insignificant gun regulation, entitlements earned from civic duty, and the commemorative events that will one day mark the fiftieth anniversary of 9/11. If you were born in the decade from 1990 to 2000, this could be a letter written by your grandchild. It was originally composed for a contest.

Since the start of the twenty-first century, Shell and *The Economist* have been sponsoring annual essay contests about the future. The top winner of the first contest in 2000 was William Douglass, whose winning entry was titled *Dear Nestor*. Douglass' essay took the form of a letter between fictitious pen pals—from Ramesh (living in Dhaka, Bangladesh) to Nestor (living in Houston, Texas).

Douglass' letter struck a chord with me. Having just completed extensive scanning as part of a master's degree project in Studies of the Future, I felt as if I had been viewing the same future world. The sensation was probably intensified by the fact that, like Nestor, I reside in Houston.

When issues surrounding freedom and security were announced as the topics of the 2002 contest, I could not resist writing a reply from Nestor to Ramesh. Responding to the earlier essay was a great exercise in *futuring*. Like a sailor taking measurements at sea, bearings were checked, marking how far the world had come and how far it had yet to travel.

The winning essay in 2002 was a comforting piece, *Milksop Nation* by Jack Gordon, which compared the issues of security to sailing. All the winning essays and rules for future contests can be found at www.shelleconomistprize.com.

After reading Nestor's letter to Ramesh, try writing a letter yourself to or from someone in the future. You never know where it might lead you.

11 January 2051

Dear Ramesh,

I enjoyed your last letter about life in Dhaka, Bangladesh. I'm sorry for not writing back sooner. I have been very busy. In addition to my schoolwork and stuff I usually like to do, I am preparing to take part in several events that will be held in remembrance of the fiftieth anniversary of September 11th. Have you studied how that day changed the course of world events?

In my Cultures Class, we studied Bangladesh as a leading example of change in the early twenty-first century. We were taught that your country was one of the first to benefit from the globe's taxes, by improving water quality and other infrastructure. Climate changes threatened the area then. The country was considered progressive in the region, for handling disputes more peacefully and accepting women in Parliament sooner.

I am not surprised by your observation that you have many foreign visitors. With world-managed rainforests, transparent security, and the Chinese Republics so near, the area receives a great deal of attention. You are rightfully proud of what economic and environmental reforms have been accomplished in your world region. Bangladesh is an esteemed Muslim country.

Like you, I take many of my lessons and interscholastic exams over the Network. I also attend classes at the Academy for Peaceful Space, a campus located just outside the gates of United Space Associates. You have probably seen the "USA" company logo on the Moon Station. United Peoples operates specialized training academies all over the world, on a variety of international issues. There are some academies near you that provide special security certifications. Several companies in your town of Dhaka offer the best computer security programs in the world.

Do not be impatient about your lessons. You will find a

program that is right for you. My cousin is in a program that specializes in food safety. He is learning to identify genetically modified foods that are targeted to affect specific ethnic groups.

I am surprised you prefer working more then studying while you are this young. I am encouraged to be a community volunteer but am not allowed to work for wages yet, unless my mom gives up the stipend she and other women receive to care for others. Does your mother receive a stipend to care for you? My Aunt Andrea says, "There is no place in the world as secure as the arms of a mother." I think she stays home because she cannot get a decent job. She did not register for Civic Duty.

I understand why your mom says the expression "country" is outmoded. The transition from national sovereignties to autonomous Bank Zones was apparent to most citizens by 2020, after Asia settled disputes. Having seen boundaries redrawn all over the world, U.S. citizens finally find it less difficult to accept the twelve statistical zones here. It is not like our country disappeared. It is accrued as regions report to the Globe Federation, just as counties, states, and countries meld together. The boundaries were established to respect cultural regions; make security manageable; reduce our targetability as the lone supra-power; safeguard data; and increase our representation in Globe governance.

Do you think the UN will drop "Nations" from its name in favor of the term "People", when the voting structure changes? We are discussing this in Current Events. Non-Governmental Organizations (NGOs) are frustrated with the restrictions placed on their demonstrations. They think elections will strengthen their input into world governance. Democratic reforms have continued to gain momentum ever since the United States replaced the Electoral College with the popular vote. I guess if the proposed voter literacy requirements are adopted, then every country will want their schools and students to get serious about education. People here still resist the mandates put forth by the chief of the North American Trading Block (NATB) because they did not elect her.

My history lessons explained that the formation of regional blocks was accelerated by economic woes and legislation early in the century. I find revisionist history about that era interesting, especially when it compares the establishment of new tax structures to events that took place centuries earlier during the reign of Philip the Fair (1285–1314). In part, computers made it easier to monitor transactions and implement an environmentally sound tax system using the industry classifications introduced earlier by the United Nations. Consumers switched hastily to the digital economy too, panicked by false rumors that bio-contaminants were spread on paper currencies.

By the way, I collect regional coins. If you want to swap, just be sure they are sealed after being disinfected. Do you collect anything?

My history teacher remembers when the transition to near fully electronic payments forced underground economies to the surface. She was scared and did not want to be drafted to squelch civil disturbances. My teacher was not the only person who was afraid class warfare would spread then, but that seems almost ridiculous now. I had to write a paper about the transition. Here it meant fewer people could afford a maid, yardman, or nanny. The cost of building stuff or owning a house increased then, too. But labor reforms and other changes directed by ministerial governance appeased most people. That's when our region finally began to link earnings to value; coordinate personnel services across industries; and divest pension and health-care options from employers.

To answer one of your questions, "Yes, I am a citizen," and a very patriotic one at that. Our citizenship taxes are minimal compared to the consumption taxes, tenant service fees, and charity tithes that are collected.

My ancestors emigrated from Iran in the 1960s. Texans just assume I am Hispanic because of the way I look.

In your last letter you also asked if I had been given any genetic enhancements. No, I was not. I passed the prenatal screening required by the Regional Genetic Bank.

Instead, I was given a nanoplant for dexterity when I was eight. Now I am great at karate! My parents considered implanting bioidentification chips, too. Humph!!! Sometimes it feels as if people think we are sheep that might get lost. Are your parents like that, too? I'm glad mine decided biochips weren't necessary. Our finger and DNA prints are stored in our Zone Identifications anyway. And like most kids, I wear a Connector that helps keep me out of trouble.

Your virtual chaperone, Jacob, sounds fantastic. I am not surprised you have Siliconite friends. Countries that did bio-experiments before agreements were enforced are ahead, just as ours was once ahead in nuclear technologies. Would you be allowed to upload Jacob's persona into a robotic bodyguard?

My closest friends are Carbon-based. I can rely on them to help if I am in a jam.

To stay connected with my folks, I use the "Big Brother" Connector. It lets my parents know where I am. That is a feature some kids do not like. I do not mind. My limits are so liberal that exceeding them would be dangerous. With a connector, I can also summon the Polizia anytime I need them.

A friend of mine used the newest Connector, a "Baby Brat," to transmit pictures of illegal drug use in progress, but the justice panel won't accept what he transmitted unless he testifies, too. My sister carries the "Big Sister." It warns her if a convicted offender is nearby. Can you believe people once thought robo-droids would fly around to protect everybody?

Do you use Connectors? I heard some countries still

do not let people have safety devices—not even radios or
haz-mat suits in dangerous factories. They are afraid
equipment could be used to overthrow their government.

In our region, people even own guns. Dad says, "Guns
would have been banned completely when hunting
declined, except companies decided it was a useful skill for
some employees." Dad would not hunt without their
sponsorship. It is too expensive, especially having the car-
cass checked for diseases. Carrying weapons is inconve-
nient, too, unless you have the new sonic bullets. Most
places monitor their entrances, but our family joined a
private club, so going out is not too dangerous.

Monitoring equipment is a big deal in my city because
we have a huge port and lots of factories. I am glad our
Ship Channel is closely monitored. No Cain Blasters have
ever been intercepted here, but our beaches are sure
cleaner. The Zedlav Incident would not have happened if
that ship had been inspected here where security is con-
centrated. Of course, our scientists cannot detect all bio-
hazards.

With government and individuals using monitors
everywhere, I feel safe from all types of violations. Still, I
share your frustration about digital images. Sometimes
you do not know what is and is not real. Ever since a
friend of mine had an unauthorized picture distributed, I
can empathize with cultures that say your soul is stolen if
you allow yourself to be photographed.

Is it true that burqa robes are now popular there? Do
people wear them to protect their privacy? Or because
they are required to be worn? Did Asia adopt the privacy
standards of the North American Trading Block or the
European Union?

Why are you fascinated by pirated Schwarzenegger
movies? I am not allowed to watch his violent movies.
Once I snuck out and saw a truly flippin' flick—*The
Matrix*. Can you intercept rogue broadcast transmissions?
If mom finds out I watched violent entertainment, she

makes me watch real suffering, like films from Unre-
formed Africa.

My favorite thing to do is read books. My family saved
some, including a collection of quotes published about
one hundred years ago. I have been reading about patrio-
tism in preparation for the 9/11 commemorative programs.

That old book of quotes has five pages about "Liberty"
and "Freedom," but not even a heading for "Security."
They believed a moral life of faith was secure.

If you cannot find a free quote database, I will send you
some. Patrick Henry's quote about bad men and good citizens haunts me. It seems the American founder could
foretell the issues churning during the Wars of Terror.

We were taught terrorists struck America in 2001 for
being decadent. Then why did attacks not stop after
decency reforms? Requiring offensive Internet sites to
identify themselves with "xxx" or "R17" extensions was
one easy compromise.

If terrorists were really angry over allies, would Peacekeeping headquarters have been a more important target
than the World Trade Center (WTC)? Among the hundreds of WTCs throughout the world, it seems obvious
now why they elected the one in New York first. After
repeated economic attacks, fiscal reforms were crucial.

Can you imagine the outcome if military actions had
been construed as religiously motivated? Eliminating references placing God in our government was inevitable
then. The Liberty Rights of 2007 were a courageous testi-
mony to freedom, an example for the rest of the world,
dignifying God's gift of Free Will. While no one "makes
the religion" here either, zeal to distinguish Church from
State and protect us from extremists nearly extinguished
the free flow of ideas. Instead, Plato would be pleased
with the dialogues occurring in our communities.

Only one quote in that old book practically integrated
the ideas of security and freedom. Paraphrasing Joseph

Cook, he said that "safe freedom" consists of four things: liberty to govern oneself; necessities to meet physical needs; opportunities to learn; and conscience to do what is right. While no region has yet perfected these ideas, I (an admittedly arrogant Texan) believe my region has come close. As we say in Texas, "It's a state of mind."

I am in an All Boys Choir that will debut a new anthem at the commemorative services that will be held throughout this year. To help us comprehend the tragedy in New York, our choir recently toured downtown Houston.

Business districts are dispersed across the city of Houston, which has proven a fortunate design. Our group could not go into many offices, but we could access City Hall, the biblio-net-heca (new library), and some stores. Offices, not damaged and demolished by the 2043 Hurricane, look like huge fortresses. They dwarf City Hall. We could not go into the tunnel system because the emergency air masks and showers were being inspected that day.

We did have our pictures taken in front of the Unity Memorial. Every major city in the world where citizens are committed to Peaceful Unity has one of these statues. Does yours? The new anthem we will sing also proclaims that peace provides security. Do you believe that?

Reflecting upon our history, I have realized our predecessors could not trade freedom for security. The biggest challenge our ancestors faced was naming what they feared most. Fears can then be coped with using reasonable applications of technology, knowledge, and conscience.

Security is best maintained by allowing informed individuals to decide the risks they are willing to take within limits formed by self-governed societies. Our world—free of deprivation—is the product of a just society where security is freedom.

I hope my preoccupation with world events and

philosophies has not offended you. Please write again. I promise to share a different passion in my next letter.

I prefer traditional handwritten letters even though they can be difficult and expensive to transport. They are more private than electronic exchanges and promote stronger, reflective relationships. With honest, firsthand sources, we are less likely to be misled by propaganda put forth by the Assumption machine. Thank you for being my pen pal.

Cordially,
Your Buddy in Houston,
Nestor

## EXERCISE

Indicate your reaction to ideas mentioned in the letter from Nestor.

| 1 | 2 | 3 | 4 | 5 | 6 |
|---|---|---|---|---|---|
| STRONGLY AGREE | | | | STRONGLY DISAGREE | |

1)  Climate changes threaten areas of the globe.

2)  We are responsible for improving water quality and infrastructure only in our nation.

3)  My grandchildren and I will take lessons or inter-scholastic exams over a network.

4)  I can identify the academies that provide training in international issues.

5)  The exploration and development of space should be a commercial endeavor only.

6)  My country provides the best possible training for security professionals.

7)  Genetically modified foods could affect ethnic groups differently.

8) Children should be allowed to work for wages if they want to.

9) Young people should be required to participate in community-service projects.

10) Women should receive stipends to care for dependents.

11) Political boundaries are often redrawn.

12) The operation of government can change without changing physical boundaries.

13) The future will be dominated by democratic reforms.

14) There are two things you can count on. One of them is taxes.

15) A fully digital economy would force underground markets to the surface.

16) Parents should monitor their children with electronic devices.

17) Children who use electronic devices like the "Big Sister" or "Baby Brat" are safer.

18) Sonic bullets are not fatal.

19) My favorite thing to do is read books, in both paper and electronic formats.

20) There are many World Trade Centers around the globe.

21) "Safe freedom" requires liberty, necessities, opportunities, and conscience.

22) Security is more important than freedom.

23) Freedom is more important than security.

24) In the future, no one will handwrite letters.

25) My opinions would change if some of these statements were slightly reworded.

# FLOATING CITIES: WHERE DO YOU WANT TO LIVE TOMORROW?*

Patrick G. Salsbury

Design Scientist/Founder, Reality Sculptors

Imagine what it would be like if your parents wouldn't let you move out of their house when you felt the time had come. Perhaps you wanted to move away for college, or a job, or to start a new family, but they insisted you could do all of that right there—in your room, in their house. Imagine there was no age at which they would let you move out, and they wanted you to stay there for the rest of your life. How would that make you feel?

On a personal level, everyone knows this would be a recipe for disaster. Yet on a national/global level, the thought of how to let a colony or subgroup exit gracefully is commonly forgotten by people running the parent government. (Witness the endless and often bloody struggle for independence of the Basques, the Kurds, the Palestinians, the Tamils, and others intent on creating their own nation.)

Both individuals and nations seem to go through a period when they feel they have grown up and wish for their own independence from their parent(s). They want to see if they can make it on their own and have their own ideas about how they want to do things. Additionally, some people (though by no means all) seem unable to get along with their neighbors.[1] Indeed, both individuals and nations tend not to like the neighbors closest to them (though they are indifferent to those farther away).[2]

When you begin to think about it this way, suddenly many of the conflicts we hear about in the daily news start to make (a bit) more sense. If it were a family-level problem, many conflicts would be avoided by letting the disgruntled family member have his or her independence and letting him or her move out. Similarly, longstanding animosity toward a neighboring family can be solved by one of the families moving away.

In the past, this was easier for dissident groups, too, because much of the globe was only lightly populated. The problem today is that nations have expanded to explore and lay claim to (the land of) the entire planet, and newly formed groups do not really have anywhere to move.

Until we reach the technological levels necessary to provide cheap and easy access to the unlimited resources of space, we are going to need to come up with other ways to get along, or we are going to see an endless stream of terrorist attacks as people decide to fight over their differences, rather than pursue their dreams.[3]

My essay proposes a novel approach to the growth-related problems outlined above: A distributed matrix of hundreds (or thousands) of cities that float on the oceans, holding physical life-support technologies and high standards of living constant across all cities, and making slight variations in the social fabric from city to city, based on local resident preference.[4]

This is not so much a blueprint for any one vision of utopia but rather a plan for a testing laboratory to allow individuals and whole societies to find their own versions of utopia using the scientific method on a grand scale.

Why bother? Because by floating cities on the ocean, you necessarily put a buffer of several hundred or thousand miles of ocean between differing ideologies, so we can hopefully avoid the sort of frictions brought about by close proximity. My general idea is to let people of a similar mind live near one another, away from those who might have problems with their way of life, whatever it may be.

A major difference between floating cities and traditional landlocked cities is that once land cities become established and grow to their respective boundaries, they really aren't going anywhere. They have reached maturity, although they continue to age. Eventually, some areas get run down and go through stages of urban renewal.

My floating city model, however, offers a radical departure. The design is based upon a simple biological model that has been in use for billions of years: cell division. As a sea-based city grows, it will draw energy and nutrient resources from the sun, wind, and sea. It will produce more physical area for its growing population and more economic opportunities.

However, unlike a grounded city, a floating city can self-replicate, then split apart. It can go through a process of "budding" to produce smaller "seed colony" copies of itself, and these may split off and float away in a new direction, both physically and ideologically. Rather than letting a city grow beyond its social or physical carrying capacity, and suffering through waves of crime, unemployment, social dissension, or overcrowding, the people of a floating city can simply decide to start a new colony at sea (or move back onto land) according to their new definitions of a utopian goal for their society.

The implications are fairly profound. No more need for wars of independence. No more need to fight over occupied zones of control. No more fighting over so-called holy land, because a floating city will likely be drifting around and not tied to any specific locale. No need for rebels fighting against powers-that-be. No more innocent people blown up on their way to work. Just an amicable shaking of hands, and a few thousand like-minded individuals hop onto a seed colony and head out to learn if they can make their idea of utopia work.

The general idea is to create a controlled laboratory environment, where you hold most of your variables constant and change just a few things. In this case, we attempt to hold life-support and living standards constant (and high) for all people.[5] Once adequate life-support needs have been established at a high standard of living for all people, everywhere, continuing social failings can no longer be blamed on poverty, inequity, and so on. The ideas that knit together the individual societies may then be examined in a rigorous way, and we can begin to explore the ideologies that either make a society function well or do not.

In this thought-experiment, "high standard of living" could not be defined as "the way many Americans live today," for that would spell ecological disaster when replicated across the globe and across billions of people. Rather, in this case, we should strive for a standard of living higher than common in the United States or other industrialized nations.

We need to create environments where everyone has enough personal space, food, water, sanitation, energy, shelter, education, health, and time to pursue their ideas of fulfillment and growth. This should be done without being wasteful, without polluting the environment, and while using the latest advances in technology and knowledge to actually repair the damage done to the planet during the twentieth century.

(Although this may sound far-fetched and impossible, it isn't. Those interested in learning how are recommended to read the book *Cradle to Cradle* by William McDonough and Michael Braungart and to watch the accompanying video, *The Next Industrial Revolution*. Both resources provide an eye-opening and exciting glimpse into available technologies and design methods that will quite literally change the world we live in, for the better.)

An example may help to illustrate the scale we're talking about. The open ocean in the Tropics has about 70 million square miles (181,300,000 sq km) of area. If you were to suppose that each floating city required one thousand square miles (2,590 sq km) of ocean resources (wind, sun, wave energy, mariculture, etc.) to support itself, then you could fit about seventy thousand of these cities into that area. At 150,000 people per city, that's a potential population of 10.5 billion people (or 1.75 times the current population of earth), just on the oceans, just in the Tropics! With numbers like these, it becomes apparent that overpopulation isn't really an issue but intelligent use of resources certainly is.

Once you have the physical infrastructure of a few of these self-supporting, eco-friendly floating cities in place, you can then begin to make slight variations in social structure, and can explore controversial issues that have proved complicated in the uncontrolled, often very densely populated environments of current cities, states, and nations.

Would you like to live in a certain type of political system? Or with a specific religion? (Or no religion?) What about guns? Legal or not? Drugs? Abortion? Race? Gender? Sexual orientation? How about a community made up of a people with a similar so-called disability? A city where most people are in wheelchairs, or are deaf, will greatly differ from one where most can walk and hear. An all-gay city, a city of gun owners, a city of legal drug users.

Suddenly, those people who are used to being a marginalized minority find that they are the majority. How will that change their society? Will they be able to achieve their vision of utopia after having removed "the oppressive yoke of (fill-in-the-blank)" that has kept them down for centuries? Or will they become oppressors themselves? (Hopefully not.)

A crucial thing to keep in mind during this thought experiment is that participation in this proposed laboratory environment is completely voluntary. This isn't a proposal for an enforced ghetto where minorities are made to go off and live only with "their own kind." But rather it is a haven to which they may flock by choice, to be with people of similar mind-sets.

The goal is to reduce friction as much as possible by letting each group pursue their own idea of utopia, without the interference of detractors. Of course, anyone who doesn't want to go may continue to live in our current societies and land-based cities. This isn't a plan to replace the existing world, just to expand the options and possibilities for those in the world.

Some people may question the idea of going to live in a place where everyone agrees with you. They may insist that it is better to stay and fight for your "rights" in the place where you are unhappy. Not only does this leave you unhappy, but it is also liable to make the other people around you unhappy. Two groups of unhappy people do not a utopia make.

To quote Dr. Timothy Leary:

> There is only one political criterion by which you can judge a country. Does it allow free exit? Does it imprison its people in the hive or does it allow self-selected egress? No matter how repressive the regime, if it permits dissidents to leave—it is a free land. Frontiers are genetic escalators. Those rebels who refuse to leave the hive, who stay to overthrow the Dictator, are by definition dumber than the evil they wish to replace. [6]

Each floating city will have its own local constitution with the rules of that group. To make sure everyone in any given city is still pretty happy with what they have signed up for, there should probably be some sort of mandatory "happiness index" rechecked every year, if not more frequently. Perhaps there could be a system in which citizens (who will probably vary with age based on different societies) are required to sign and renew their adherence to the local constitution yearly. In essence, they are signing the Social Contract that we often hear about but usually never see in our current societies.

Times change, people change, laws change. What sounded like a great idea a few years ago might not actually be so good in practice. For example, perhaps you have a family now, and all those guns everywhere in the Free-Gun Society are making you nervous. If you're not happy, then you're not in your personal utopia, and under the provisions of "The Floating Cities Experiment," you should be able to pursue your happiness elsewhere. It may be another floating city, or it may be back on the mainland.

There should be some sort of travel-agency type of service that can help you find what you're seeking. If everything in your current location is perfect, except for the guns, then maybe you need City No. 429, rather than No. 287 where you live now. Socially identical but no guns.

The astute reader may notice this idea is not new. In fact, this proposal is based upon the same principles of our country, when the Founding Fathers drafted the Constitution. This was when the United States had a small population, virtually limitless resources (per person), and room for all to grow and pursue their dreams. (Compare that with today, where some neighbors may complain if you don't mow your lawn or if you paint your house the "wrong" color!)[7]

Will letting people live their dream lead to social failure? Possibly. In fact, in some cases, there is a good probability, which is valuable to know. For example, a city of fifty thousand democratic, pro-drug, pro-choice, antigun people might thrive, while a city of fifty thousand Communist, pro-drug, pro-choice, pro-gun people might not. Holding other things steady, we have two variables. Was it the Communism or the guns that caused one city to fail? Or some combination of both?

Even if (or especially if) some cities don't make it, this will be useful information for the rest of humanity—specifically in the next fifty to one hundred years, as we begin to move off the planet and out into space. This utopian testing lab will hopefully provide pointers to what types of social systems tend to produce extremely happy people, only so-so people, or extremely disgruntled people. And that information may mean the difference between life and death when a ship carrying 100,000 people or more heads off into the interstellar void.

It should also prove useful to people still living here on Earth.

* An earlier and different version of this essay appeared in Arthur B. Shostak, ed., *Viable Utopian Ideas: Shaping a Better World* (Armonk, N.Y.: M.E. Sharpe, 2003), 99–101. ("Distributed Floating Cities: A Laboratory for Exploring Social Utopias")

NOTES

1  Both of these points seem to hold true irrespective of the specifics of race, cultural background, geographic location, class, wealth, religion, political ideology, or a host of other parameters. In fact, though these various parameters are often blamed for the

inability to get along with neighboring families/cities/states/
nations, often they are not the root cause of conflict but merely a
convenient difference that allows one group to take sides against
another group.

2   Timothy Leary, Ph.D., "The Neuro-Geography of Terrestrial
Politics," *The Intelligence Agents* (Tempe, Ariz.: New Falcon Publications, 1979), 39–44.

3   On life off-planet, see related essays in the fourth volume in this
series.

4   These are topics covered in more depth on the floating-
cities mailing list and the Reality Sculptors Web site at
http://reality.sculptors.com/—where you can find archives of
past discussions or join in future ones.

5   In a biology lab, it is common to see dozens or hundreds of
petri dishes with the same substrate of nutrients, while some
other factor is manipulated in a controlled fashion. In this proposed planetwide sociology lab, the petri dishes would simply
be large-scale floating cities that are each home to 5,000 to
150,000 people.

6   Timothy Leary, Ph.D., "Winter 1977 Tucson Lecture—America
Is Where You Find the Change Impulse," *The Intelligence Agents*
(Tempe, Ariz.: New Falcon Publications, 1979).

7   The notion that human beings will fight with one another as
part of their basic human nature is so pervasive and accepted as a
natural law that it appears constantly (and without question) in
our stories, movies, and even our games, either as the prime plot
device, or as a narrative backdrop against which the action plays
out. The "Civilization" and "FreeCiv" computer strategy games
draw from history and pit cultures (players) against one another.
The sequel game to "Civilization," called "Alpha Centauri," and
the space-game "Freelancer" are both set in a futuristic, sci-fi
setting, after humanity has begun the migration to other star systems, yet still falls back to the familiar models of one faction
fighting against another. It is so ingrained in us that no one even
questions the basic assumption that we're never going to get
along—even eight-hundred-plus years in the future. (Hopefully,
we can do better.) Despite these assumptions, all of the above
games, and especially the "Sim City" series, provide an excellent
"virtual-society" lab and a way for individuals to quickly play-test

different arrangements of physical and social parameters similar to the floating-cities experiment outlined in this essay. They are a far cry from the complexities of a real society, filled with real people, but they do help to train your mind in trying to grasp some of the many variables that have to be juggled at once to try to achieve balance and harmony, and are well worth exploring.

## REFERENCES

Salsbury, Patrick G. "Distributed Floating Cities: A Laboratory for Exploring Social Utopias." Edited by Arthur B. Shostak. *Viable Utopian Ideas: Shaping a Better World*. Armonk, N.Y.: M.E. Sharpe, 2003, 99–101.

The Whole Future Catalog, Floating Sea Cities section: http://reality.sculptors.com/cgi-bin/wiki?WholeFuture/ Cities_That_Float_On_The_Sea

## FURTHER READING

### Biological Wastewater Remediation

Dharma Living Systems
    www.dharmalivingsystems.com/
Ocean Arks International
    www.oceanarks.org/

### Principles of Eco-Effective Design

McDonough, William, and Michael Braungart. *Cradle to Cradle*.
    New York: Farrar, Straus and Giroux, 2002.
McDonough Braungart Design Chemistry
    www.mbdc.com/
*The Next Industrial Revolution*—companion video to *Cradle to Cradle*
    www.thenextindustrialrevolution.org/

### Technical Background/How to Build It

The Floating-Cities mailing list

http://lists.sculptors.com/mailman/listinfo/floating-cities
Biorock—Electrodeposition and Reef Building/Restoration
　http://www.biorock.net/
The Creation of Free Settlements
　http://www.islandone.org/Settlements/
Wolf Hilbertz, Coral Process/Electrodeposition
　www.ar.utexas.edu/Staff/swaffar/Hilbertz_2002/
Natural Energy Laboratory of Hawaii Authority
　http://www.nelha.org/
Oceana—A Proposal for a New Country
　http://reality.sculptors.com/~salsbury/Oceana/Oceana.html
Seament Research
　www.stanford.edu/~erlee/seament/Seament.htm
SeaSteading—Homesteading the High Seas
　http://web.gramlich.net/projects/oceania/index.html
Seastead.org
　www.seastead.org/
Diary of a Seasteader
　www.livejournal.com/users/seasteading/

## Offshore/Floating City Projects

The Celestopea Project
　www.celestopea.com/
The Living Universe Foundation
　www.luf.org/
Oceania—The Atlantis Project
　www.oceania.org/
Principality of New Utopia
　www.new-utopia.com/
Sargassia
　www.sargassia.com/
The Venus Project—The Redesign of a Culture
　www.thevenusproject.com/city_sea.htm

Courtesy of The Venus Project
Designed by Jacque Fresco and Roxanne Meadows

# Part Three

## CHALLENGED ABROAD

*I see great days ahead [for America],
great days possible
to men and women of vision.*
—Carl Sandburg

Two essays in this section, each strong in having a novel perspective and an encouraging closing forecast, explore the "hot button" matters of globalization and foreign policy. The first essay contends that its subject is poorly misunderstood and unfairly maligned. Nine insightful forecasts and five more personal ones lead up to a constructive wake-up call. Similarly, the second essay challenges the reader to ask how much of a part should traditional American values have in our foreign policies, especially those values grounded in religion. A case is made for America's serving as a more explicit, if also sensitive employer of religious values, the better to assure that we represent the best of our Founding Ideals. For as a forecaster explains, "Our common future depends on creating an international system built on a foundation of inclusiveness, cooperation, and consent."[1]—Editor

NOTE

1 J. Orstrom Moller, "Wanted: A New Strategy for Globalization," *The Futurist*, January–February 2004, 26. See Johan Norberg, *In Defense of Global Capitalism* (Washington, D.C.:

Cato, 2003). A passionate rebuttal of the case made by anti-globalists; see also Andrew J. Bacevich, ed., *The Imperial Tense: Prospects and Problems of American Empire* (Chicago, Ill.: Ivan R. Dee, 2003). Twenty essays that seek to bring ordinary Americans back into the discussion of U.S. foreign policy, this time seen through the prism of empire.

# ◼ Essay Ten ◼

# GLOBALIZATION AND YOU

## Medard Gabel
Founder, BigPicture Consulting

Globalization has changed your life. That's right. What you wear, eat, listen to, watch, drive, get sick from—and even whom you date—have been influenced by or even determined by globalization.

Check out the labels of your clothes. Look where that computer, CD player, cell phone, television set, and skateboard was made. This wasn't always the case. Ask your parents. Ask your grandparents. There was a time, and not too long ago, when a great deal of what you owned was not made in China or some other place overseas. Globalization made this possible.

Check out your classmates. Chances are they are from all over the world. Many have parents for whom English is not their first language. You or some of your classmates may also be in this category—and it is not by accident. Their presence is due in large part to the forces of globalization.

Do you like sushi? How about Indian, Thai, Italian, or Ethiopian food? How about world music?

Just about everything in your world is a product of the most powerful force in our world—globalization. And not only is your present world influenced and expanded by the powers of globalization, your future is also going to be seriously influenced by it. Your future is going to be a product of your vision, values, decisions, and the options that globalization has furnished you. And luckily, at least from my perspective, those options are increasing.

**WHERE DO WE STAND?**

Let's take the simple *Globalization Intensity Test* and see just where we stack up on the globalization continuum. Answer the following questions and then total up your points at the end.

**Globalization Intensity Test**

1) Where were the shoes you're wearing made?
   A. U.S.
   B. non-U.S.

2) Where was the shirt you're wearing made?
   A. U.S.
   B. non-U.S.

3) Do you own a computer?
   A. No
   B. Yes

4) Where was your computer made?
   A. U.S.
   B. non-U.S.

5) What was you favorite movie last year? Where was it made?
   A. U.S.
   B. non-U.S.

6) How many languages do you speak?
   A. 1
   B. 2 or more

7) How many people do you know who were not born in the United States?
   A. 0
   B. 1-2
   C. over 3

8) How many contemporary musicians from outside the United States and Europe can you name?
   A. 0
   B. 1-2
   C. over 3

9) What kind of car do you drive (or want to drive)?
Where is it made?
A. U.S.
B. non-U.S.

10) Have you been outside of the United States? To how many countries?
A. 0
B. 1-2
C. over 3

For all "A" answers, give yourself one point. For all "B" answers give yourself two points. For all "C" answers, give yourself three points. Then see how you line up.

10 points    Low
15 points    Medium
24 points    Maximum

The higher your score, the more integrated you are into the global, rather than the national economy and culture.

> *It has been said that arguing against globalization*
> *is like arguing against the laws of gravity.*
> —United Nations Secretary General Kofi Annan

**DEFINING TERMS**
So what is this thing we call globalization? If it is so powerful, important, and pervasive, why aren't we studying it in school?

First of all, globalization isn't a "thing." It is not a noun; it is a verb. It is a process. And one with a long history—and, like you, a great future.

It is critical to our understanding of the process of globalization to realize that it is as old as Earth itself. It is not some new invention of the Information Age or a product of Madison Avenue advertisers trying to get you to buy the latest fashion accessory.

One thing that happens to anything that shows up on our

planet, be that single cell life, human beings, or technology, is that it spreads around the world. We don't find air just over Chicago and water all scrunched around New York or Los Angeles. The very names given to our planet's air, water, and living resources—atmo*sphere*, hydro*sphere*, bio*sphere*—have a geometry to them that suggests they are part of the entire planet. Simply put, when something shows up on our planet, it soon finds its way around the entire planet. That is a form of globalization.

The fossil record shows that early humans showed up first in Africa. (All of us come from Africa.) Approximately one hundred thousand years ago these first humans, following migrating herds of animals, went north into Europe, Asia, and eventually, approximately 14,000 to 20,000 years ago, found their way into the Americas. We spread around the world.

"Human migration" is just another name for the globalization of our species.

When we developed technology, it also spread around the world. The primary technological drivers of globalization have been and still are transportation and communication. As our transportation advances—the wheel, paved road, horse-drawn wagon, motor vehicle, sailboat, steamship, railroad, airplane, and jumbo jet—showed up, they both spread around the world and they "shrunk" the world. That is, as the speed of transportation increased, it cut the time it took to get from here to there.

These new transportation technologies created increasing capabilities and capacities for individuals, entrepreneurs, students, governments, armies, and tourists—thereby transforming the world. The communications advances of the alphabet, printing press, mail service, telegraph, telephone, radio, television, computer, and Internet had an even more profound impact on our world.

As technology progressed from the wooden sailing ships of Magellan's era to the steel steam-powered ships of the 1850s, the time it took to travel around the world was reduced from two years to two months. Further transportation advances reduced this time to two weeks as the internal combustion engine-powered airplane showed up, and then to two days with the advent of the jet. The space shuttle now makes the journey in less than two hours.

In summary, the process of globalization has made your world:

* One world (rather than a bunch of remotely isolated groups);
* One environment (so now pollution from China or anywhere else can impact your air);
* One market (so now you can buy products from all over the planet in your neighborhood store);
* One technology base (so now CD players and computers are available throughout the globe, to anyone who can afford them);
* One labor pool (so that workers in Malaysia now compete with workers in Maine);
* One financial pool (so the multinational corporation and even your city can now borrow money from banks in Chicago, London, Hong Kong, or Tokyo);
* One culture pool (so now we can all enjoy music, dance, and art from all over the world);
* One disease pool (so now we can all catch the latest version of the flu—or HIV or SARS—days after it shows up somewhere in the world);
* One crime pool (so organized crime is now international in scope);
* One problem pool (all our problems are now global because everything is connected to everything else in our global economy).

### ECONOMIC GLOBALIZATION

This is the form getting all of the attention these days. The integration of our local, regional, and national economies into one global economy, and the painful transitions, for many people, that are caused by this process are what get many people stirred up. When your father loses his job to a worker in India or China, there is pain. When the factory in your town shuts down because it cannot compete in the global market-place, and leaves people you know without the means of sup-porting themselves, you may become angry and want to do something.

Economic globalization, the integration of our local economies into a global economy, involves a lot of change, and change can bring about an increase in our options and wealth, as well as economic pain. On the whole—that is, from a global perspective—globalization is a clear plus. According to the United Nations Development Program, the world's wealth has improved more in the last fifty years than in the previous five hundred years. Globally, we are better off. China alone has pulled more than 300 million people (more than the entire U.S. population) out of abject poverty.

Locally, we have people who *are* getting hurt by some of the sudden changes brought about by economic globalization, but globally we have more people living as "haves" than ever before.

Economic globalization is measured by the flows of goods, services, people, money, ideas, and problems across borders. Globalization interconnects everything with everything else—in ever more effective and profound ways, linking you to the world. Globalization has made the world "smaller." It substi-tutes speed, connection, and complexity for distance.

People have become embedded in larger and richer webs of interdependence—providing you with more options for school, play, friends, and (eventually) work. Your competitors for that job (or position in the college of your choice) are increasingly not from just the school down the road, or in the next state, but from Germany, Taiwan, India, Brazil, and China.

Whether you realize it or like it, you are now (in addition to your citizenship in your local community, town, state, and nation) a global citizen.

## ... AND YOU

So what does this have to do with your future? Where is all this taking us? What does it mean to you? Here are a few notions as to where globalization is taking us:

1) The process of globalization is not over. The world is going to become even more integrated, "small," fast, and fun.

2) Economic globalization will continue to cause disruptions and painful transitions in our local economies.

3) Economic globalization will result in increasing wealth for the world.

4) Your music (and food, clothes, games, names) will continue to be influenced by musicians (and chefs, fashion designers, game designers, parents) from all over the world.

5) The odds of your dating and marrying someone from outside your community, state, and country are increasing.

6) Communications and transportation technology will continue to advance. It will continue to become easier to get in touch with almost anyone, anywhere—just as long as that person has access to the same technology.

7) Your knowledge of the rest of the world will continue to increase—especially as the rest of the world continues to play a bigger and bigger role in the United States.

8) Your knowledge of the "have-nots" in the world will continue to increase as their plight, and the difference between what they have and what you have becomes clearer.

9) People from around the world will continue to adopt technology that allows them to communicate with people in other parts of the world. Cell phones, computers, and Internet access will continue to proliferate and expand in usage.

Here are a few notions as to what this all means for you:

1) Globalization is creating more options for you. Think about going to school, either for a semester, or longer, in another country. The experience of a "foreign" country is crucial to your becoming an informed global citizen—and to your becoming more competitive in the global job market.

2) Globalization is creating more competition, as well as potential friends, for you. Students from all over the world are now your peers.

3) Globalization has made the world more fun. It is now almost as easy to travel abroad (and often cheaper) than it is to travel across the United States.

4) Globalization has made the world more dangerous. Terrorists (and SARS and other viruses) are able to travel, too. HIV and sexually transmitted diseases are a global problem with which you need to be informed and extremely cautious.

5) The more you can learn about the world, the more fun it will be—and the more opportunities you will have. Learn all you can about the world while you are in school, especially from your friends who have lived in other parts of the world.

Globalization has changed your life already. It will continue to make changes tomorrow and into the foreseeable future. We have the choice to *use* it or be used by it.

## ■ Essay Eleven ■

# SHAPING TOMORROW'S FOREIGN POLICY

### Chris Seiple
President, Institute for Global Engagement

As you live in the mightiest country the world has ever known, you and your generation share responsibility with the rest of us for how that power is wielded. Your descendants a century from now—and beyond—will curse or bless the impact *your* generation will have had on the United States and the world. So, it is time to think seriously about America's role in the world, and in particular, about the near future of our foreign policy.

How to start? Our first step is to take a long, hard look at our global context, at who we are, and who we want to be. For example, and to get personal for just a minute, I turned thirty-six this year (2004). I now represent the median age in the United States. And, even more significant, the median age in this country is projected to hover around thirty-six all the way out to 2050.[1]

This plateau of early middle age will persist even as much of the developing world continues to get younger (think "youth bulge"), and the rest of the so-called developed world gets noticeably older (think "Old Europe"). By 2050, the median age in Europe may move from thirty-eight (currently) to fifty-three. The world's population may increase 18 percent by 2015 (from 6.1 billion to 7.2 billion), and 95 percent of that growth is expected to occur in the developing world, mostly in chaotic, sprawling, massive cities.

The United States will be positioned between these age extremes, possessing—hopefully—a collective outlook that is neither young nor old, but *youthful*, for the next two generations (the fifty-plus additional years of your average life span).

*Youthfulness* is not defined strictly by age. It combines the best of the young (vision and vigor) with the best of the old (moderation and maturity). It is a trait Americans must carefully nurture as they recognize and take responsibility for the vast power (cultural, political, military, economic, etc.) that we have in today's world.

High schoolers like you can help the United States make the most of this—make the most of our sustained demographic youthfulness (2004 to 2050). We can achieve a responsible youthfulness in international engagement, one that balances our obligations as a superpower with our values as Americans. In this way, tomorrow's foreign policy can engender the goodwill and security we want and need.

The United States, thank goodness, has the vigor of a young nation (despite being the oldest liberal democracy on the planet). Ours is a nation of innovation, and we lead the world in Nobel Prize winners (three times as many as the next country). Ours is a culture of initiative, and we spend more on research and development than any other country. We are also a nation of new ideas (more patents are applied for each year in the United States than in the entire European Union, which has 150 million more people than the United States). No wonder that since 1995, 60 percent of the world's economic growth has come from the United States.

At the same time, we have unprecedented military might. There is an overwhelming gap in weaponry, not only with our readily dwarfed opponents (see Panama, Haiti, Serbia, Afghanistan, and Iraq) but also with our envious allies. It would be easy to conclude that we can do what we want, simply because we can. But this is as wrong as it is easy to formulate, and we base tomorrow's foreign policy on it at our great peril.

In high school courses that had you read about our nation's founding and our Constitution, you learned that "balance" is our national philosophical watchword—*balance* of powers, *balance* of majority rule and individual rights, *balance* of ambition and restraint, and so on. U.S. foreign policy, however, is at risk of becoming unbalanced—of allowing youthful vigor to out-weigh seasoned wisdom.

Exercising power—especially the mind-boggling variety we alone possess—does not necessarily earn international respect. In fact, possession of such extraordinary power can tempt us to choose arrogance and ignorance, resulting in an international backlash and putting us at unnecessary risk.

While much anti-Americanism masks petty jealousy, many thoughtful people across the planet now tell pollsters that they consider the United States the greatest threat to peace. In global politics, perception can and commonly does become reality. International opposition to the United States is linked to the perception that we are far too brash, rash, and trigger-happy; that we possess many of the worst characteristics of the young and few of the best characteristics of the old.

To earn genuine and lasting global respect, our foreign policy must turn toward responsible *youthfulness*. Neither unchecked macho self-interest, nor undisciplined naive idealism will serve our best interests. What is needed is a new ethos of service rather than one of (self-deceptive) supremacy.

Remember the demographics that matter, for example, "thirty-six years." In the United States, I am still relatively young, while for an average baby girl born in Sierra Leone today, thirty-six years is her entire life expectancy.[2] AIDS-ravaged South Africa will probably witness a decrease of its population from 43.4 million to 38.7 million over the next eleven years, producing millions of orphans. By 2015, chronic malnutrition may increase by 20 percent in sub-Saharan Africa. In such environments, the educated are fleeing the places that need them most, emigrating in droves.

If the United States is to capitalize responsibly on its youthfulness for the next half-century, it must act with more moderation and maturity, stewarding the vision and vigor of U.S. citizenship in a global neighborhood. It will be hard work!

Which brings me to our second step: I believe foreign policy takes place at the intersection of values and interests. What is most interesting about the twenty-first century is that this intersection is dominated by religion.

Think about our core American values. More than 80 percent of us believe in God. But we believe in a way that allows each and every soul to choose—or not choose—their faith *freely*. It truly is remarkable, a tolerant civil society that dates back to the establishment of religious freedom in the Rhode Island colonial charter of 1647 and 1663.

Now consider our interests. Religious freedom is actually involved in everything from economic negotiations with China to informing our response to a global terrorist insurgency that has hijacked Islam and is using it as an excuse for murder.

More specifically, if in the near future there is not freedom of choice in China, including freedom of religious choice, China will never develop into the capitalist trading partner we need it to be. Similarly, if in the near future moderate Muslims do not seize back their faith—if they do not soon reclaim its ancient tradition of tolerance—then we will only continue to suffer terrorist attacks.

Consider the recently approved constitution in Afghanistan. It makes Afghanistan an "Islamic Republic" whose laws must be consistent with Islam. Yet, there are provisions for religious freedom and the rights of women. Time will tell how this plays out in practice, but certainly a tolerant public square in Afghanistan is critical to its longevity; that is, if it wants to avoid the return of the Taliban.

All we can really know is that the longest yet surest road to stability and security will come from a culturally congruent form of tolerance—something we Americans can never impose, only enable. The same goes for Iraq. Freedom to choose there might mean a freely elected, Shiite-dominated state. At the end of the day, the best we can hope for is a process through which all people choose to at least tolerate each other, and maybe, if we are lucky, respect one another. The United States can create the opportunity and, hopefully, set the example, but it cannot choose for other peoples.

You, as a teenager, can decide even now if you favor a *youthful* U.S. government that champions *freedom* at home and abroad; one that really grasps the constructive part that religious values can play in improving international affairs. If the United States is to shine as a respectful civil society over your lifetime, we must account for the fact that while we may not, the rest of the world often thinks of religion and politics in the same breath. If the creation and implementation of our foreign policy is to be realistic, we must do the same.

## SUMMARY

The United States is an eight-hundred-pound gorilla on the world stage. Accordingly, we urgently need to consider how our country actually "plays with the other kids in the park." We need to envision and promote a near future that embodies the best of religion *and* the best of politics if it is to truly reflect American values and interests. If you begin thinking about this scenario now, and soon act on its behalf, your great-grandchildren in 2105 will have good reason to smile with warm approval, thankful that you were their early-twenty-first century ancestor.

## NOTES

1 Unless otherwise noted, the statistics found in this essay are based on *The Economist* Special Report, "A Nation Apart," 7–8, 12, 14 November 2003; the National Intelligence Council's (NIC) 2000 Report: Global Trends 2015 (available at www.cia.gov/cia/reports/globaltrends2015/index.html); and a speech given by John L. Helgerson, chairman of the National Intelligence Council, on 30 April 2002, to the Denver World Affairs Council and the Better World Campaign ("The National Security Implications of Global Demographic Change," available at www.cia.gov/nic/NIC_speeches.html).

2 Annual Report, World Health Organization, as reported by Richard Waddington, "Life Expectancy in Retreat for World's Poorest-UN," Reuters, 18 December 2003.

FURTHER READING

**See also by the Author**

Short piece on how persecution results in instability, 21 February
2003, www.globalengage.org/issues/2003/02/safe.htm

Op-ed on the Iraq War's strategy and what our troops would
encounter, 24 March 2003, www.fpri.org/enotes/20030324.
americawar.seiple.baghdadspring.html

Three-thousand-word piece on the role of the United States in the
world and the need for a grand strategy, 25 April 2003,
www.globalengage.org/issues/2003/04/sustainment.htm

Op-ed on the role of education in preparing our leaders for today's
security complex, 21 May 2003, www.govexec.com/dailyfed/0503/
052003db.htm

Three-thousand-word piece on the nature of today's war—a global
counterinsurgency—and religion's role therein, 2 September 2003,
www.globalengage.org/issues/2003/09/religion.htm

Op-ed on religious freedom and realpolitik in Afghanistan and Iraq,
5 November 2003, www.globalengage.org/issues/2003/11/ftp.htm

# Part Four

## WAR AND PEACE PROSPECTS—TOMORROW

*The Difficult is that
which can be done immediately;
The Impossible is that
which takes a little longer.*
—George Santayana

Five essays in this section explore the possibilities of war or peace in the near future. Risks here get higher with ever successive announcements (or rumors) of still another country joining the exclusive "club" of nations in possession of nuclear weapons. Because "... a radioactive Armageddon doesn't extend the option of any good places to hide ... [we] belong to an endangered species, never more than thirty minutes from an appointment with extinction."[1]

The first essay cautiously forecasts where tomorrow's battle lines might be drawn, the role of India and China, the significance of netwars (as in the Iraq War), and some options for countering the threat of *Jihad*. The second essay makes a case for several earthy and promising steps to improve the chances of peace throughout the Middle East (topics include the Palestinian-Israeli conflict, relations between Syria and Israel, the democratization of the Islamic world, and developments in Iraq). The third essay hones in on the Iraq situation and artfully lays out the possibilities. (An informed journalist forecasts that "free nations will win in the world war on terror ... [for when a combination of democracy and prosperity] brings a better life to people of the greater Middle East, the basis for hatred and terror will erode, and the suicide bombers will pass from the scene.")[2]

125

Two more essays shift the focus to peacemaking per se and help a reader imagine what a world without war might resemble, and how we might—actually—get there (slowly and haltingly). They raise hope that "future generations, when they have tasted the fruit of a culture of peace, will recognize almost intuitively that peace is their right."[3]—Editor

NOTES

1 Lewis Lapham, *Theater of War* (New York: The New Press, 2002).

2 William Safire, "Creeping Democracy," *New York Times*, 22 March 2004, A23. See also Charles Kurzman, "Bin Laden and Other Thoroughly Modern Muslims," *Contexts*, Fall–Winter 2002, 13–21.

3 Douglas Roche, *The Human Right to Peace* (Ottawa, Canada: Novalis, 2003), 230. See also Jim Garrison, *America as Empire: Global Leader or Rogue Power?* (San Francisco, Calif.: Berrett-Koehler, 2004). Urges Americans to ask this future-shaping question: What quality of empire can and should our country become? Garrison recommends one that renders the need for empire obsolete.

# ■ Essay Twelve ■

# FUTURE TENSE: WAR AND PEACE 2015

## Marilyn Dudley-Rowley and Thomas Gangale

*Editor's Note: Marilyn and Thomas are social scientists who, when they were barely out of their teens, served in the U.S. military, and are interested in issues of war and peace. I asked them to give a sketch of "things to come" on the battlefields and around the peace tables over the next five to ten years.*

*Marilyn*: Battle lines today are, and in the foreseeable future will be, blurry in new ways. When you and other teens came into the world in the mid-to-late 1980s, the Cold War was still in progress. We and our allies were butting heads with the Soviet Union and its allies, the West *versus* the Eastern Bloc in a seemingly never-ending smack-down match.[1]

In a world of clear boundaries, despite fear of worldwide nuclear war and "them against us," at least we knew where we stood. Today, the battle lines between enemies aren't as clear—and haven't been since the Cold War came to an end in 1989. This is what we face as the first decade of the twenty-first century segues into the second.

Some nations that were once enemies are now on the same side, as in the case of the United States and Russia. Yet many of the old animosities stay the same. A good example: bad relations between India and Pakistan that go back decades. But now, with nuclear warheads and missile capabilities on both sides, the possibility of a nuclear exchange ups the ante, making their conflict even tenser for those of us who look on from ringside.

*Thomas*: If you want to try to draw the battle lines of the near future, take a look at Samuel Huntington's *Clash of Civilizations* approach. He outlines how sub-Saharan Africa may become more conflictual with predominantly Islamic countries.[2] Japan and Russia may become more hostile toward each other. Russia and Islamic countries may suffer more frictions. Western countries may be at loggerheads with Islamic countries. Relations between the West and China may become more conflictual. India and its allies may become more hostile toward China and Islamic countries.

At the same time, however, it may get pretty cozy between India and Russia, and between Latin American and Western countries. In fact, you can consider Latin America as part of the West in Huntington's framework. Also, as China becomes more powerful, Japan may drift from the U.S. sphere of influence and seek an accommodation with China.

*Marilyn*: Some of the conflict and cooperation Huntington foresees is owing to historical momentum. For example, Japan and Russia have had territorial disputes for a century. It is obvious that Western countries and Islamic countries have long been, and are currently in active dispute.

But, some conflictual relationships will evolve from both older historical ties and new events playing out in the here and now. For example, Russia is concerned about Caspian Sea oil and gas reserves and the avenues of transport of these reserves through Islamic countries in Central Asia. So, what does Russia do? Being an Orthodox Christian country, it teams up with its historical allies and fellow Orthodox countries Serbia and Greece to offset Islamic Turkish influence in the Balkans, and it gets cozy with Orthodox Armenia to get it to restrict Turkish influence in the Transcaucasus.

Turkey has historical ties with all of the Central Asian republics, like Uzbekistan and Turkmenistan (which are not only Islamic but also ethnically and linguistically Turkic). Because those republics sit on top of oil and gas reserves, which are of interest to Turkey and Russia, Russia binds those republics to it, and keeps Turkish influence out by deploying military forces under the guise of protecting those countries.

*Thomas*: Turkey, however, is a traditional friend of ours, one that has hosted a number of U.S. military facilities since the early Cold War period. It also wants into the European Union. As if this didn't complicate things enough, as the biggest oil consumer on the planet, we eye those *same* oil and gas reserves that Turkey and Russia want to control. Add in our conflicts in Iraq and Afghanistan, and this *really* gets interesting.

So you can see how fuzzy the picture is today, as compared to yesteryear's Cold War world, one defined mostly as "them" and "us." That leads me to ask: In this stew of hot, cold, and lukewarm relationships, does the United States remain the world hegemon?[3]

*Marilyn*: Oh, you mean, do we Americans stay the top dog in the world system of societies? Well, I'm afraid that *could* change. About the mid-twenty-first century, China might rise up to challenge the United States for that position, but then toward the end of the century, India might try to challenge whomever is on top. This is going to be a very hard challenge for teens today who must confront this world. They see the United States as the center of the universe, as we did when we were growing up. What will be their response when Beijing is the new center or New Delhi?

*Thomas*: Whoever stays or gets on top would seem to depend on where technology takes us and on the demands of population. China has about 20 percent of the world's population, and India's population is nearly that big.

*Marilyn*: Just because China or India takes center place on the world stage in the twenty-first century does *not* mean either of them will be enemies to the United States.

*Thomas*: Indeed. A debate is raging in national security studies regarding the future utility of military power in an increasingly interconnected, globalized world. A lot of smart people realize that if you go to war with your trading partners and customers, your sales numbers take a serious beating.

What is feared, instead, are what we call *netwars*.[4] Over the next ten or so years, old-style "shooting wars," those that nation-states used to fight with higher-tech weaponry and international-ized troops, are likely to be increasingly upstaged by the war-like efforts of nonstate-sponsored networks of ordinary citizens.

Two major networks are already at one another's throat: One is manned by supporters of capitalist sameness, by champions of global corporations that want us to buy the same brands (*their* brands) the world over. In *Beverly Hills Cop III*, the side-kick of Detective Axel Foley (played by Eddie Murphy) asked: "You want to die for your Camry?" Well, these are the people willing to die for their Camries, and their Nike sneakers, and their Chevron gasoline.

An opposing network draws on stateless organizations that seek to insulate and protect their own distinctive cultural and religious identity. Members hate all that threatens their ways. Evil, in their fierce view, emanates from McDonald's-like Western homogeneity, with its ultra-modern sameness, and its sponsorship by Western-origin corporations.[5]

(Fanatical fundamentalists are not the only holders of this view. There are also some Americans who are greatly opposed to the way things are. "Eco-terrorists," for example, already target and burn stores and S.U.V. showrooms.)

*Marilyn*: This *Jihad* will undoubtedly become a major military force. And it does not need very sophisticated weaponry. Instead, for years ahead terrorists will rely on the human factor, on volunteers who improvise with available hardware to make their deadly point (as when they strap on a suicide belt of nail-studded bombs).

This poses a very special danger—one that exposes the drawbacks of missing the signs. Our corporatized world has come to rely on unmanned drones and spy satellites. Because it neglected the human factor, we were caught flat-footed on 9/11. Those willing to die before allowing the erasure of their cultural and religious lines will increasingly rely instead on taking over airliners, on driving suicide car bombs, and on arming child soldiers with AK-47s. To meet this new challenge we *must* bring the human factor back in.[6]

*Thomas*: Absolutely. Technical intelligence—spy satellites and drones—can tell you where there are buildings and bunkers. They cannot tell you what is *inside* a man or woman's head, what he or she is thinking and planning. For that you need human intelligence—not spy gadgets but *spies*.

We need to develop a human resource pool with the necessary skill sets. We should encourage high schools and colleges to teach more foreign languages and geography. We need to get young people involved in learning languages other than English and learning how to understand other cultural horizons.

We also need to merge the human factor with the high-technology factor. Defense labs are studying ways to enhance cognition and perception, to integrate human skills with machine skills. We may soon be able to use cutting-edge electronics to monitor what is going on in several battlefield venues at once. Genetic engineering (mentioned elsewhere in this book) might soon produce better warriors with faster reflexes. Nanotechnology might eventually produce better weaponry and military gear, making it possible to manufacture the necessary materials in battlefield environments.

*Marilyn*: There are and will still be some dangers from nuclear devices being weaponized by terrorists and rogue states. But it is the *stateless network*, not the *state-launched nuke*, that now puts the front lines everywhere—and with an instantaneity that surpasses the trajectory of a guided missile. Not only are the front lines on the soils of our homelands, but now they are in our hearts as well.[7]

**QUESTIONS TO PONDER**

1) Why is the United States the primary consumer of petroleum? How do some of the other nations compare in their usage of petroleum?

2) What would happen if India or China developed an automobile industry of their own that demanded heavier usage of petroleum products than they use today?

3) Where are Uzbekistan, Turkmenistan, Kyrgyzstan, Kazakhstan, and Tajikistan, and what are their boundaries with Russia, China, and other countries?

4) Which foreign languages should schools and colleges teach for the foreseeable future to increase human resources for the world we now live in?

5) Are there ways we could preserve cultural and religious identities in a world where boundaries have come to mean less than they once did?

## NOTES

1 This Cold War has been going on since before Thomas and I came into the world. If teenagers really want to get a handle on the paranoia and the stakes that each side faced, they should find a copy of the remake of *Fail Safe* starring George Clooney.

2 Another challenge will be the growth rates of African populations. They are growing faster than Chinese and Indian populations. But there are other demographic factors to consider in Africa than overall population increase. In some countries, the HIV infection rate is 25 to 50 percent. The generation most sexually active is also usually the most economically productive: young and middle-age adults. Yet, in Africa they are sick and dying. This is destroying what little economic power Africa had and is also devastating its culture. African grandparents are spending most of their efforts caring for their dying adult children and trying to raise their grandchildren. Working jobs to support both, they have little time left for passing on their cultural heritage to their grandchildren. We may actually see population crashes in some of these countries. Who knows, if the nations of Africa could organize, they might join in the race for world hegemony. But that possibility may have to wait for the twenty-second century. It will be interesting to see Africa beginning to move in that direction—perhaps with warm relationships with India.

3 Anyone who wants a picture of "the future enemy" should read Benjamin Barber's ideas about *Jihad vs. McWorld*. In his framework, there are now two forces in tension, both relatively unrestrained by the rules and regulations, by the sovereignty of any nation-state. First is the combined force of many

antimodern groups (like Muslim fundamentalists) looking
for cultural and religious identity in a world of too-fast
communications and too-rapid transportation. Second is a force
that reflects a hyper-modern world being made ever more
homogeneous by the machinations of capitalists unrestrained by
national controls. Barber believes these contradictory forces will
breed outlaws who will buck and strain the sovereignty of
nations. In response, nation-states will demand creation of global
governance, a kind of world government, to police the outlaws.
Yet, major challenges to global governance remain that won't be
easily overcome. Oddly, while these two forces are in tension,
they actually depend on each other. They used to say in the
nineteenth century that the "sun does not set on the British
Empire," the world hegemon of that century. Now, the sun does
not set on McDonald's. You can literally find the golden arches
on every continent with the possible exception of Antarctica.

4  Sociologist Manuel Castells even goes further in talking about
the irony of the interdependence of marginal and terror groups
and those they wish to destroy. He says that people who would
have just been sucked into the growing homogeneity of the
world have managed to join in endeavors to keep cultural and
religious differences *different*. They have managed to do this
through the high-tech instruments of a homogenizing world.

5  *New York Times* columnist Thomas Friedman, the source of this
idea, is another one of those who illustrate the tension of a world
of many differences becoming a world of sameness. Now,
because I use college students, some still in their teens, to do
research for me, I show them how making contact with such
groups is just a "Google away." But, I warn them not to talk to
anybody on those sites. I don't want us drawing the attention of
potential terrorists *or* the Department of Homeland Security.

6  At the same time, Al Qaeda ironically owes a debt to the very
things it wishes to destroy. As Benjamin Barber notes, Osama bin
Laden would have been just a desert rat without the corporate
media that have made him a superstar. He would not have been
able to move his money around the world to bankroll terrorist
operations without the high-tech financial systems that ignore
national boundaries. Want to join in the efforts of a terrorist or
marginal organization? It's just a Google away.

7  See, in this connection, the seminal work of Manuel Castells:
   Manuel Castells and Martin Ince, *Conversations with Manuel Castells* (Oxford U.K.: Polity Press, 2003).

## REFERENCES

Barber, Benjamin R. *Jihad vs. McWorld: Terrorism's Challenge to Democracy*. New York: Ballentine Books, 1995.

Castells, Manuel, and Martin Ince. *Conversations with Manuel Castells*. Oxford, U.K.: Polity Press, 2003.

*Fail Safe*, (Movie), 2000. Director: Stephen Frears. Actors: George Clooney, Richard Dreyfuss, Noah Wyle, Brian Dennehy, Sam Elliott, James Cromwell, John Diehl, Hank Azaria, Harvey Keitel, Norman Lloyd, and Don Cheadle.

Friedman, Thomas L. *The Lexus and the Olive Tree*. New York: Anchor Books, 1999.

http://hfetag.dtic.mil/. The Web site of the United States Department of Defense Human Factors Engineering Technical Advisory Group.

Huntington, Samuel P. *The Clash of Civilizations and the Remaking of World Order*. New York: Touchstone, 1997.

Nolan, Patrick, and Gerhard Lenski. *Human Societies: An Introduction to Macrosociology*. 9th ed., Boulder, Colo.: Paradigm Publishers, 2004.

## ■ Essay Thirteen ■

# FUTURE OPTIONS FOR THE MIDDLE EAST: THE ART OF PRACTICAL PEACEMAKING

### Tsvi Bisk
Futurist/Strategy Analyst

While there are far too many nominees, any list of the top challenges to our future would include four set in just one volatile area of the world, one in which high schoolers and other civilians brutally die each day. The challenges include: 1) the Palestinian-Israeli conflict; 2) the ever-present threat of war between Syria and Israel; 3) the question of the democratization of the Islamic world; and 4) the question of whether we can soon construct a *constitutional* democracy in Iraq. Nothing less is at stake in these four matters than our ability to have a future worth having.

### THE PALESTINIAN-ISRAELI CONFLICT

Palestinians and Israelis have a completely different view of peace. It is not helped along by isolated Jewish settlements in the heart of hostile Arab populations. Nor is it aided by Nazi-style anti-Semitic propaganda in the Arab media and school curricula. It is not promoted by the humiliation of Arab civilians at roadblocks. Nor is it helped by the glorification and encouragement of the *Shahid* (suicide bomber). It does not gain from a fourth generation of refugees still living in camps run by the United Nations. Nor is it aided by encouraging these refugees to believe the "right of return" to Israel is a realistic possibility.

Peace would have a far better chance if several parties—not just Palestinians and Israelis—would try to solve concrete problems, try to create practical conditions from which a "true" peace might eventually evolve.[1]

### The Refugee Problem

One of the reasons the 2000 Camp David talks broke down was over the issue of the Palestinian refugees. The Palestinian leadership affirms the "right of return" of these refugees to Israel, according to United Nations General Assembly Resolution 194. Israel counters that any such enormous influx would mean the destruction of the Jewish state and Jewish self-determination. Israelis believe that since self-determination is defined as a right in the United Nations Charter, Resolution 194 actually runs counter to the UN charter.

Many Palestinians realize there is no way Israel is ever going to give in. Yet Palestinian leaders cannot give in as long as so many Palestinians live in the squalor of refugee camps. Their Palestinian constituencies would eat them alive if they did. The solution is to make the Palestinian refugee problem a nonissue. How?

1) The European Union and the United States could join in an integrated project to generate a 10 percent annual economic growth rate in Jordan over the next ten to fifteen years. Sixty percent of Jordan's citizens are Palestinian. They constitute the largest Palestinian refugee population. Jordan has more than 90 percent literacy and greater than 15 percent of its population has a post-high school education. Economically, Jordan may be part of the undeveloped world, but sociologically it is part of the developed world.

Jordanians have the human resources to support such a growth rate over a sustained period and to become a modern middle class society relatively quickly. This would eliminate the refugee problem in Jordan and lessen grass-roots pressure on the Palestinian leadership regarding the "right of return."

2) About four hundred thousand Palestinian refugees live in Lebanon. Their camps are more internment than refugee camps. Unlike Jordan, Lebanon permits no Palestinian integration into the country. The Palestinians are not citizens and have no rights. They live in complete squalor with no hope whatsoever. Not surprisingly, this group is the most radical in regard to terror candidates and to the "right of return."

The United Nations, the European Union, and the United States could pressure Lebanon to grant them citizenship. In return, the European Union and the United States could declare these camps "tax free zones," enabling free access of all goods and services produced in the camps to European and U.S. markets. A special investment bank could be established to generate such economic activity. As with the Jordanian example, within ten to fifteen years these people would become middle class, reducing the grass-roots pressure on the Palestinian leadership regarding the "right of return."

### The Settler Problem

About three hundred thousand Jewish settlers live in the West Bank. About two hundred fifty thousand of them live on 2 percent of the land contiguous to the pre-Six Day War (1967) borders. The Palestinians have already agreed that these areas can be annexed to Israel, and in return they will receive an equal amount of land from Israel contiguous to the Gaza Strip.

The real problem, therefore, encompasses only about fifty thousand settlers.

Thousands of these settlers would be willing to leave their homes immediately if they received suitable financial compensation. These include all the settlers in the Jordan Valley, several entire settlements around Jenin, most ultra-Orthodox settlers, and many individuals in even the most ideological settlements. Many settlers are in desperate economic straits, unable to make a living where they reside and unable to afford to move.

No Israeli government is *politically* capable of buying these settlers out before a peace agreement. The U.S. government would also find it politically difficult to initiate a fund for this purpose. But the European Union could. This step combined with real pressure on the Israeli government to stop building settlements would result in a process whereby within ten to fifteen years the real number of settlers on *disputed* land would be insignificant.

### Peace and Terror

The Israeli public will be deeply suspicious of any peace initiative as long as suicide bombers continue to blow up Israelis. The nation's leadership, sensitive to constituents, will not reduce reprisals against the Palestinians unless terror ceases. These reprisals result in more Palestinian recruits for suicide bombings. Unless this cycle of violence is broken, conditions for peace cannot be created.

Terror is the keystone. Practical peacemaking requires a drastic lowering of the number of suicide bombers. The Israeli solution is what they call the "Security Fence." Only about a third of this fence has been built, and it has already resulted in a dramatic decline in terror infiltrations into Israel.

Unfortunately, the Israeli government, under pressure from the settlers, has built parts of this fence deep into occupied territory. This has much of the world outraged, and the Israelis have been called upon to cease building the fence. Of course, the Israelis will do no such thing, given the results against terror.

A solution would be for the European Union and the United States to offer to pay for the total cost of the fence on the condition that it follows the "green line" (the internationally recognized border between Israel and the Palestinian Authority). This would save Israel the $1 billion to $1.5 billion it is costing to build the fence, would negate international public opinion against the fence, and greatly improve Israel's security.

All of the above would help create the conditions necessary for peace to evolve between the Palestinians and the Israelis. Ideally, it would be better if the Palestinians and the Israelis could agree to a comprehensive peace that would establish a Palestinian state with its own "Law of Return"; giving every Palestinian the right to return to Palestine (not Israel). But this does not seem to be in the cards in the foreseeable future. So practical step-by-step peacemaking is the only alternative.

### ISRAELI-SYRIAN PEACEMAKING

Several years ago Israel and Syria were very close to a peace agreement. Israel was to give up the entire Golan Heights in return for a full peace agreement with Syria (and, by implication, Lebanon).[2] But the deal fell through. Not because of land but because of water. The Syrians wanted the border to be on the water's edge of the Sea of Galilee (the 1948 ceasefire and pre-Six Day War border). The Israelis wanted the border to be three hundred yards from the water's edge (the 1947 partition plan border).

The Sea of Galilee is Israel's largest water reservoir, and as such it has tremendous strategic value. The Israelis fear that despite a peace treaty, Syrian dissidents or terrorists would be tempted to poison the reservoir with biological or chemical weapons and bring Israel's economy and society to its knees.

How could we reduce this fear in order to create the conditions for a peace agreement between Syria and Israel? Israel could give up the entire Golan Heights (to water's edge) in return for a major desalinization project financed by the European Union that would produce water equal in amount to the water Israel draws out of the Sea of Galilee. This would not prejudice any of Israel's rights to the water of the Sea of Galilee.

Israel would have a major net gain in its water resources, a strategic reserve if the Sea of Galilee were to be damaged, and a peace agreement with Syria and Lebanon. Syria would have its land back. This must be accompanied by an end to *Hizballah* terror from southern Lebanon into Israel, which could be guaranteed by a NATO presence in South Lebanon.

### CAN ISLAM BECOME DEMOCRATIC?[3]

What is still lacking in Islam is the secular Western tradition of self-criticism and focus on the future that arose during the European Enlightenment. There has been and is no Islamic Voltaire or Jonathan Swift, and there is too great a preoccupation with the past over the future.

Without self-criticism and the consequent focus on the future, there can be no democracy. Self-criticism of necessity obligates one to focus on the future, for one does not correct

oneself in the past but only as a future project. It goes something like this: "What is wrong with us? What must we do to
correct it? How are we going to do it?"

Many Muslim intellectuals (both Arab and non-Arab) are
beginning to address this deficiency. Self-criticism coming out
of the Arab and Muslim world in the last couple of years is
encouraging and bodes well for the long-term development of
democratic habits of thought.

The next step is the concrete application of these habits of
thought in political documents and institutions that the masses
will regard as culturally accessible and acceptable. The example
below of Iraq might give some indication on how to pursue this
concrete application.

### CAN IRAQ BECOME A CONSTITUTIONAL DEMOCRACY?

The United States wants democracy in Iraq. But what kind of
democracy: majoritarian or constitutional?

Majoritarianism places no limits whatsoever on the majority
or the leaders who speak in their name. Hitler, Stalin, Mao
Tse-tung, and Fidel Castro are twentieth-century examples of
majoritarian rule. Hitler was elected in a perfectly democratic
manner and was certainly supported by the vast majority of the
German people. There can also be little doubt that the vast
majority of the people supported Mao and support Castro.

Constitutionalism, on the other hand, is essentially a limitation of the powers of the sovereign authority in its dealings
with the individual human being. The sovereign authority
could be a queen—as in Britain's constitutional monarchy—or
it could be "The People"—as in the constitutional Republic of
the United States. In both cases, the rights of the individual
human being are protected by a "Bill of Rights" against the
arbitrary passions of an individual monarch or a majority of the
people.[4]

Majoritarian democracy places no limitations on the power
of the majority; constitutional democracy does. This is *not* a
theoretical question in Iraq. The Shiites constitute 60 percent
of Iraq's population. A majoritarian democracy would give

them total control of the entire political apparatus, to the detriment of the Kurds, the Sunnis, and other minorities.

How can the Shiites achieve their just political representation without endangering the rights of the other ethnic and religious groups? Let's do a "mental experiment" and try to imagine a workable constitutional solution based upon unalienable rights of individuals and minorities and limitations of power.[5]

The Iraqi Chamber of Deputies might be composed of one hundred representatives (or more) who would be elected by voters in legislative districts divided proportionally according to population (much like the congressional districts in the United States). This would almost guarantee that Shiite representatives would comprise the majority of this body.

The Senate would be composed of thirty-six members: two from each of Iraq's eighteen provinces. This would be regardless of the population of the provinces and would almost guarantee that the majority of the Senate would *not* be Shiite. This would be similar to the Senate in the United States, which is composed of two senators from every state regardless of the state's population and which was purposely designed by the Founding Fathers to limit the power of the majority. The people would directly elect the Iraqi prime minister, almost guaranteeing that he (or she) would be a Shiite. The Senate would choose the Iraqi president, almost guaranteeing that he (or she) would not be a Shiite.

The prime minister or any one of the two houses could initiate laws. They would have to be approved by both houses and the prime minister. The president, however, would have to confirm the law. If he/she refused to do so, it would be referred to an independent constitutional court, elected by both houses. The members of this court would all have to be university-trained jurists. Only they could overrule the president's veto. Religious clerics would *not* be permitted to sit on the constitutional court.

Each province would also have its own legislature with provincial prerogatives of power constitutionally guaranteed. This would be a further diffusion of power friendly to the anti-majoritarian principles of constitutionalism.

This entire approach could find its cultural and religious justification in what we discussed above relating to the possibility of democratizing the Islamic world. Indeed it is necessary that the entire constitutional superstructure of Iraq (and other Arab and Muslim countries) be clothed in that part of the traditional language of Islam that sanctions and validates the unalienable rights of the God-created individual human being.

This supports not only a limitation of the powers of the state and the majority but also of the religious clerics. They can interpret religious law, but they cannot use the powers of the state to coerce individuals. Nothing in Islam sets clerics above any other human being.

By functioning within Muslim tradition, the West can *assist* progressive Muslims in moving the Muslim world toward constitutional democracy. Imposing democracy from without is a non-starter, and it can even be counterproductive.

This is because our natural tendency is to begin with the end; the end being democratic elections. Having democratic elections without first developing a constitutional culture of rights and limitations of power will result in a majoritarian democracy ruled by the passion of the mob and directed by religious fanatics.[6] Let's get our priorities straight: first constitutionalism and then democracy.

### CONCLUSION

Peacemaking is a serious and complicated procedure. We would all be better off if we understood that there are no magical instant solutions, only processes that should be put into place as soon as possible. What do you think?

NOTES
_____

1 The attempt to achieve a *wide* consensus about a final peace settlement has intensified the dispute rather than lessened it. The

well-meaning attempt by former President Bill Clinton at Camp David to achieve a final peace settlement seems to have contributed to the outbreak of the second Intifada.

2  This is the "Land for Peace" principle enshrined in United Nations Resolutions 242 and 338.

3  The monotheistic inheritance has given us two fundamental concepts without which democratic principles could not have developed. The first is we are all made "in the image of God" and the second is we are all descendents of Adam and Eve.

During the Peasants' Revolt in fourteenth-century England, one of the revolt's leaders asked: "If we are all descendents of Adam and Eve, why should some be more privileged than others?" The biblical idea that we are all made "in the image of God" led these Englishmen to conclude logically that "we are all equal in the eyes of God," and if we are all equal in the eyes of God, why shouldn't we all be equal in the eyes of man-made law. These biblical concepts pervaded English culture until they received their full secular expression in the American Revolution and the writing of the Constitution of the United States.

Equality before God is inherent in *all* monotheistic religions. Its most radical expression is the Muslim *Haj* to Mecca, where all the pilgrims must dress exactly alike so as to have no differentiation between class, race, or nation. The Muslim custom of *Haj*, joined with certain Islamic traditions that define the inherent unalienable rights of the individual human being, makes me more optimistic than most about the possibilities of democracy developing soon in the Muslim world.

4  The Constitution of the United States protects the individual from the majority and from the government that represents that majority.

5  I have chosen a modified Italian model joined to a modified American model for purposes of this mental experiment. The Italian model has a bicameral parliament composed of a Chamber of Deputies and a Senate, a strong prime minister, *and* a strong president capable of vetoing a law approved by parliament and the prime minister. This veto can only be overturned by the decision of the Constitutional Court, which is chosen by both houses.

6  One should never forget that Hitler attained power democratically in free and fair elections. He then used his power to destroy
   the very democracy that placed him in power. He was able to do
   this because Germany, unlike England, did not have a historic
   constitutional tradition.

## KEY TERMS

Bicameral; Camp David; Constitutional Court; Constitutionalism; European Enlightenment; *Haj*; Intifada; Kurds; Law of
Return; Majoritarianism; Mental Experiment; Peasants' Revolt;
Right of Return; Shiites; Sunnis; Jonathan Swift; UN Resolution 194; Voltaire

*[EDITOR'S NOTE: A contributor to this four-book series, after
reading the essay above, urged me to reach out for a Palestinian view.
He recommended Nada Khader, a U.S.-based director of
a nonprofit peace and justice educational organization, the WESPAC
Foundation.] She wrote:*

*"Questions to Ponder: Is there ever a situation where one country has the
right to invade another and impose a foreign system on it? How
would you feel if your town or city were occupied by foreign troops who
spoke a language you did not understand? How would you feel if they
wanted to change the government of the United States into a system
foreign to you? How would you feel if they put up a foreign flag at
your city hall or town hall instead of your flag? What would you do
about the situation? Would you be justified in taking any action or
not? How do you think Palestinians feel about living under Israeli
military occupation? How do you think Iraqis feel living under U.S.
military occupation?"*

# FORECASTING IRAQ'S FUTURE: DEMOCRACY À LA ISLAM OR IS IT DÉJÀ VU ALL OVER AGAIN?

Usha Menon, Ph.D.

Associate Professor of Anthropology, Drexel University

Residents of Baghdad rubbed their eyes in disbelief and wonder! Who would have thought a dusty morning in early April 2003 would bring this most unbelievable of sights—U.S. tanks rumbling through the streets of downtown Baghdad meeting hardly any resistance? U.S. planes had been bombing Baghdad for days, and rumors had been rife about an impending American entry into the city. Now it had finally happened. Iraq was rid of a cruel dictator who had oppressed and exploited its people for nearly twenty-five years.

Nothing could have symbolized the end of Saddam's brutal regime more than the toppling of his larger-than-life-size statue in central Baghdad's Paradise Square, and the kicking and stomping it received from ordinary Iraqis, venting their rage.

But what does the future hold for the people of Iraq, now that Saddam is gone? Forecasting is, in and of itself, risky business; real life has a way of proving even some of the soundest forecasts wrong. And forecasting a country's future is, perhaps, even more foolhardy.

Keeping this caveat in mind, a sensible forecaster would speculate that there are at least two possible scenarios in Iraq's future—the first, the emergence of a democracy, albeit one with an Islamic flavor, and the second, persistent sectarian violence ultimately leading to the seizure of power by a despot little different from Saddam. Each scenario is to be viewed as an approximation, as a prototype, and the real events that do unfold are very likely to be some variation of these prototypes.

## ETHNIC AND RELIGIOUS DIVISIONS IN IRAQ

Of all the people in Iraq, Shiites have perhaps suffered the most under Saddam. The world over, the followers of Islam are broadly divided into two sects—the Sunnis and the Shiites. In terms of numbers, the Sunnis are unquestionably the dominant group. Broadly speaking, 85 percent of Muslims are Sunnis, and the remaining 15 percent are Shiites. In most places, Sunnis predominate over Shiites; but Iran and Iraq are exceptions. Thus, in Iraq roughly 60 percent of the population is Shiite; of the rest, about 20 percent are Sunni Arab and 20 percent Sunni Kurd. Despite their numerical superiority, Iraqi Shiites have never enjoyed political power.

Since the creation of Iraq by the British at the end of World War I, Sunni Arabs, though a minority, have wielded political power over the Kurds to the north and the Shiites to the south, and have repressed both groups with impunity. Saddam and his Baath Party have been only the most recent Sunni Arabs to do so.

In 1988, suspecting the Kurds of separatist tendencies and insurgent activities, Saddam used poison gas against them, killing thousands. In 1991, after the first Gulf War, with the active encouragement of the first Bush administration, the Shiites rose up against Saddam Hussein; but with no material help or support from any external power, the rebellion was quickly and violently crushed by Saddam's forces. Since then, the Shiites have been quiescent, distrustful of the United States, and by extension, the West.

In contrast, the Kurds, though similarly oppressed, have, since the 1991 war, enjoyed considerable autonomy. The no-fly zone patrolled by U.S. and British planes under a United Nations mandate had seriously limited Saddam's ability to administer and control southern and northern Iraq. While the Shiites in the south had not capitalized on these restrictions placed on Saddam, the Kurds had and, in the process, gained substantial, even if informal, sovereignty.

However, both Iraqi Shiites and the Kurds have taken heart from the latest U.S. invasion of Iraq. Finally, freedom from

Sunni domination appears to be within reach. But the early days of American occupation belied this hope, as U.S. forces appeared to be unprepared for the work involved in administering postwar Iraq. Anarchy prevailed. The cities and towns of Iraq were without electricity and water. Revenge killings against Baath Party members occurred with impunity. Looting was rampant; people looted offices, schools, hospitals, and museums, carrying away furniture, machines, bathroom fittings, and even wiring and pipes.

But today, more than a year later, matters are slowly improving, although the level of violence continues to be high. The most hopeful sign, of course, is that Iraq seems to be taking the first steps toward becoming a democratic and pluralistic society, symbolized by the signing of the interim constitution.

## IRAQ'S INTERIM CONSTITUTION

The twenty-five members of the Iraqi Governing Council signed the interim constitution in March 2004. Acknowledging Iraq's ethnic and cultural diversity, it declared that Iraq would have a "republican, federal, democratic, and pluralistic" government. On June 28, 2004, the Americans handed over power to an Iraqi interim government vested with full sovereignty. This Iraqi government was formed through consultations with the Iraqi people and will govern according to the interim constitution. Within six months, Iraq is supposed to hold elections to the national assembly. A transitional government will take office after the elections.[1] The national assembly will have the primary task of framing Iraq's permanent constitution, which will then be voted upon in a national referendum. If the constitution is adopted, elections under the permanent constitution will be held for a new government, which will take office no later than December 31, 2005.

## IRAQ'S FUTURE
### Scenario One: An Islamic Democracy

For many Muslims across the world, the idea of a secular Western democracy is anathema. One of the fundamental principles of Islam is *tawhid* or the Unity of God. In terms of political philosophy, *tawhid* implies that when Muslims affirm the Unity of God, they are affirming the sovereignty of God. By identifying the sovereignty of the people as a defining element of secular Western democracy, such a political system violates the sovereignty of God, or *tawhid*, and therefore, for a Muslim, commits blasphemy.

But there is a way out of this impasse, and it derives from another fundamental principle in Islam—that of the vice-regency (*khilafah*) of man. Thus, people can govern themselves but only through accepting the sovereignty of God and only as God's vice-regents. Muslims do not reject the idea of a democracy; they only insist that it be framed within the worldview of *tawhid*; that it be an Islamic democracy.

As many observers of the Islamic world have noted, during the waning decades of the twentieth century, there was a resurgence of Islam. Interestingly enough, this resurgence has occurred in tandem with pro-democracy movements across the Middle East—in Egypt, Algeria, Sudan, and Iran, for example. In the 1970s, after nearly two decades in power, many of the governments in these countries had failed to deliver on their economic and political promises. The dominant ideologies of the mid-twentieth century—nationalism, socialism, and secularism—had not served their purpose. The hopes and aspirations of the nationalist struggles had given way to cynicism, political instability, and severe economic problems. Disappointed and restive, people began turning to Islam as an alternative source of inspiration. And new Islamic organizations came into being.

Like the Muslim Brotherhood established in Egypt in 1928 by Hasan al-Banna and the Jamaat-i Islami founded by Maulana Abu al-Ala Maududi in India in 1941, these newer organizations were not reacting to Western ideas and influences but were proactively seeking to create social institutions and political structures that could operate in an "authentically Islamic way,"[2] within the context of a modern, rapidly globalizing world. Thus, in the contemporary Muslim world, Islamization and democratization occur concurrently—the voice of the people is the voice of Islam (*vox populi vox Islam?*).

However cautious the Iraqi Governing Council may be of explicitly articulating the place of Islam in Iraq's polity, there is no point pretending that a secular Western democracy, if tried, will be anything but short-lived. Given its overwhelmingly Muslim population, the only kind of democracy that is likely to be self-sustaining and long-lasting in Iraq is an Islamic democracy.

### Islamic Political Discourse

If an Islamic democracy is what lies in Iraq's future, does Islamic political discourse have the resources in terms of ideas and concepts that would enable and encourage the development of democratic institutions? The answer is yes and no. On the one hand, the Islamic concepts of *shura* (consultation), *ijma* (consensus) and *ijtihad* (independent interpretation and judgment) are central to Islamic political tradition, and they are certainly essential to the practice of democracy anywhere.[3] But, on the other hand, Islam does not recognize the separation of powers between the legislative, executive, and judicial branches, and, other institutions that could limit the arbitrary exercise of power by the state are relatively undeveloped.

As far as freedom of expression is concerned, Islamic political theory has the concept of *ikhtilaf* or diversity of opinion. It reflects the historical circumstances in which Islam spread. As the Islamic world expanded during the seventh through the tenth centuries, it encountered a wide variety of peoples and cultures. As long as these newly converted peoples abided by the fundamental principles of Islam, Muslim rulers and jurists were willing to accept disagreement on subsidiary matters.

In addition to the concept of *ikhtilaf*, Muslims have traditionally been able to challenge the actions of their rulers on the grounds that they deviate from or violate the fundamental tenets of Islam. In fact, it is the duty of devout Muslims to rise up against unbelief and ungodly rulers. But the concept of *fitnah*, or civil disorder, places stringent limitations on the exercise of this right. In Islamic political thought, *fitnah* is the most dreaded of all situations, something to be avoided at all costs, and Islamic religious scholars (the *ulema*) are absolute in their condemnation of it.

Historically, Islamic religious scholars have always supported the ruler against the people because they interpret any challenge to authority as a precursor to civil disorder. In the context of a democracy, this is particularly unfortunate because, in Islamic political thought, religious scholars are the only people who can legitimately question and limit the power of the ruler.

### Two Models: Iran and Sudan

Given the constraints and the potential for democratic functioning in Islamic political discourse, what would be the shape of Iraq's Islamic democracy? There are two possibilities: Iran and Sudan. Both countries exemplify political Islam in action.

If Iraq were to follow Iran's example, it would enshrine the primacy of Islamic law in its constitution and impose a government of religious clerics. Iraqi democracy would be an odd mixture of authoritarian rule and popular, even contentious, political participation. There would be regular elections to the national assembly but no multiparty system and no effective opposition. Heated debates would take place in the national assembly. The press and media would be sharply critical of the government.

But all this dissent and debate would take place within the parameters set by Islamic ideology. Like Iran, Iraq then would simultaneously affirm the possibility of an Islamic democracy and highlight the authoritarian nature of Muslim political institutions and practice.

If Iraq were to follow Sudan's example, Islam's primacy may not be enshrined in the constitution, but it would still exert enormous influence on political affiliation and participation. Multiparty elections would be held. But the multiparty system would soon deteriorate into sectarian politics—demonstrating Islam's power, not to unite, but to divide.

Iraq's problem, then, would be the same as the one the Sudanese have been trying to resolve—unsuccessfully, as it happens—for the last forty years: to evolve a nonsectarian political system that is both Islamically identifiable and welcoming of secularist and non-Muslims.

In Sudan, the failure to evolve beyond sectarian politics has meant a moving back and forth between short-lived coalition governments and slightly longer-lasting military regimes that are then overthrown by popular movements. Given Iraq's recent history, Iraqis do not seem to share the Sudanese ability to oust military governments. If Iraq were to adopt Sudan's path toward democracy, it might end in a dictatorship—a case of déjà vu, all over again.

### Scenario Two: Sectarian Violence and the Rise of Despotism

Undoubtedly, the worst scenario would be for Iraq to collapse into unremitting sectarian violence. The divisions among Iraqis—ethnic (Arab versus Kurd) and religious (Sunni versus Shiite)—are sufficiently bitter and longstanding to make such a scenario a real possibility.

The worst aspect of such persistent sectarian violence would be if Iraqis were to welcome a return to authoritarian rule because that was the only way of ensuring the security of life and property. Then, the occupation and all that it has cost in terms of lives lost and people maimed would have been futile—Saddam would have been replaced by an updated version of himself.

The level of violence plaguing Iraq today—the suicide bombers, the rocket-propelled missiles, the improvised explosive devices—seems to suggest that disaffected Sunnis have been joined by foreign fighters in resisting the Americans and the British. The coalition authorities have themselves admitted that a motley group of Saudis, Jordanians, Palestinians, Yemenis, and others, belonging to an assortment of terrorist organizations, has crossed into Iraq to fight the holy war against the occupying infidels. They see the occupation of Iraq as one more assault on Islam by the non-Muslim world and one that they have to combat since none of the governments in the Islamic world will. The danger, of course, is that if sufficient blood is spilled, it could tip the country in the direction of an endless cycle of revenge killings and sectarian violence.

Some observers have spoken of Iraq erupting into civil war, and ultimately, breaking up into three separate areas—the Kurdish north, the Sunni center, and the Shiite south. Such a breakup, it is thought, would reshape the Middle East. According to this logic, the Kurds in Syria, Turkey, and Iran would seek to unite with Iraqi Kurds to create an independent Kurdish nation, and the Shiites to the south would be tempted to join with their coreligionists in Iran.

But the history of the Middle East during the latter half of the twentieth century suggests that such a radical redrawing of national boundaries is unlikely to happen. Most of the national boundaries in the Middle East are relatively recent, having come into being in the early and middle part of the twentieth century. Yet, they appear to possess remarkable resilience.

Most of them were decided by the politics of colonialism and nationalism, scant heed being paid to ethnic and religious differences. And yet, they have been extremely influential in defining identity, leadership, and social and religious movements in this region of the world. Thus, the Iran-Iraq war that lasted for eight long and bitter years from 1980 to 1988 did not see Iraqi Shiites rise up to aid and assist their Shiite brothers in Iran. Their religious identity as Shiites took second place to their national identity as Iraqis.

However, if sectarian violence were to persist, there is the likelihood that a leader could emerge, strong enough to quell the violence, stop the bloodshed, and maintain order but entirely lacking in a commitment to democratic principles. In the long run, such an effective, but undemocratic leader could evolve into a despot as ruthless as Saddam—another case of déjà vu, all over again.

## CONCLUSION

It is extraordinarily difficult to forecast Iraq's future. This essay has laid out a couple of likely scenarios. Ultimately what happens depends on the wisdom and foresight of the people in charge. Men like Ayatollah Ali al-Sistani, the most respected of Shiite leaders in Iraq today, wield enormous power in such situations. Sistani had been pressing for national elections to be held without delay. Relying on the numerical superiority of the Shiites, he was apparently hoping that a Shiite-dominated government would take political control in Iraq.

The unexpressed fear in most observers' minds is that once the Shiites come to political power, Sistani might try to bring about an Iranian-style Islamic Revolution in Iraq and never relinquish power. If he did so, then one of the scenarios sketched out in these pages would come to pass: Iraq would have an Islamic democracy very similar to Iran's. To what extent the lives of ordinary Iraqis—Shiites, Sunnis, and Kurds—will have been improved in the process is, of course, another matter altogether.

NOTES

1 Known as the Transitional Executive Authority, it will consist of a Presidency Council and a Council of Ministers, including a prime minister. The Council will include the president and two deputy presidents, and will be elected by the national assembly as a group. The Council will nominate the prime minister and, on the recommendation of the prime minister, it will also nominate the Council of Ministers. They, in turn, will need to be confirmed in a vote of confidence by the national assembly.

2 John Esposito and John Voll, *Islam and Democracy* (Oxford, U.K.: Oxford University Press, 1996), 5.

3 The Islamic concept of *shura*, or mutual consultation, is tied to the Islamic principle of the vice-regency, or *khilafah*, of human beings—ordinary men and women delegate their authority to the ruler, and he seeks their opinion in all matters related to the governance of the state. Similarly, *ijma*, or consensus, is the

cornerstone of Islamic law. In Islamic legal traditions, consensus has played a critical role in the validation of laws as well as in building a corpus of legal interpretations. Historically, however, the consensus only extended to the community of religious scholars (the *ulema*); but again, this is a flexible concept that can be extended to include all legislators elected in a modern democracy. Finally, *ijtihad*, or the exercise of informed, independent judgment, is thought to be necessary for the implementation of God's will at any time or place. According to Islamic scholars, God's will is very broadly defined, but because it is so broadly defined, God has also given humans the ability to interpret and apply it. The concept of *ijtihad* recognizes that interpretations can vary from one age to another, but it is thought to be the only way of incorporating divine guidance into the business of daily living. Indigenous to Islam, *shura*, *ijma*, and *ijtihad* are three key operational concepts that are remarkably pliant, lending themselves readily to the development and practice of democracy in the modern world. But Islamic political thought is much less flexible when it comes to the question of dissent and the role to be played by a responsible opposition, both necessary in any democracy in order to check the arbitrary exercise of power by the state.

# ■ Essay Fifteen ■

# ALTERNATIVE FUTURES OF WAR: IMAGINING THE IMPOSSIBLE

## Sohail Inayatullah, Ph.D.
### Editor, *Journal of Futures Studies*

> *War is the darkest spot on humanity's history.*
> —P.R. Sarkar*

Asking if war has a future may appear ludicrous, given that the twentieth century was one of the bloodiest ever, and that scores of low-grade wars are currently maiming and killing countless thousands. You may wonder, why even ask? Haven't we always had war? Won't we always have war?

At times, however, questioning can lead us toward a different type of analysis, possibly even giving us the means to create a future without war. To change the future, we must be able to imagine a different future. As a Lithuanian leader recently said: "Seventy-five years ago, it was impossible to imagine a post-Communist world. Then twenty years ago, we could imagine it, but we did not understand how it could practically come about. Now, we are a proud and free part of the European Union" (*Interview on Australia National Radio, August 2003*).

The impossible *can* become the possible, first by imagining, then by creating a plausible process, and bravely and persistently taking necessary steps. So, we *must* raise the question: Does war have a future? We must challenge the notion that just because war always was, it always has been.

Writes Fred Polak: "Many utopian themes, arising in fantasy, find their way to reality. Scientific management, full employment, and social security were all once figments of a

155

utopia-writers' imagination. So were parliamentary democracy, universal suffrage, planning, and the trade union movement. The tremendous concern for child-rearing and universal education and for Garden Cities all emanated from the utopia. [It] stood for the emancipation of women long before the existence of the feminist movement. All the current concepts concerning labor, from the length of the workweek to profit-sharing, are found in the utopia."[1]

Conceiving, of course, is only part of the challenge. We need to go on to create and implement social invention. Specifically, we need to devise new methods to resolve international conflicts. We need to challenge the entire notion of armed conflict, as conducted by powerful governments and weaker organizations.

To do so, we need to first analyze the multiple causes of war. Four levels of analysis can help us unravel issues and create better future possibilities. The first is the level of the litany, the unquestioned "truth" said over and over, presented day in and day out on video and television. The second is the level of the system: the historical, economic, political, environmental, and technological reasons. The third is the deeper cultural perspective: the worldview we live in. This is hard to see, as we breathe it. Just as fish do not know they swim in water, we can rarely see our worldview unless we begin a process of deep questioning. Finally, there is the unconscious story, the group consciousness.

### THE LITANY

In thinking about war and peace, the superficial analysis usually contends that if we can find and kill all the bad guys, and also destroy all the rogue nations, everything will be all right. From James Bond to Arnold Schwarzenegger to Steven Seagal, the plot is predictable. But as Mike Myers' satiric movie character *Austin Powers* suggests, evil may not only be out there, but it may also be in us. We are often—knowingly or unwittingly— complicit in evil. Hence, this vastly oversimplifying approach has awesome limitations.

## SYSTEMIC ANALYSIS

The focus here is on historical, economic, political, environmental, and technological reasons for war and peace. For example, proponents emphasize the need to rapidly transform the arms-export industry, such as by making the export of killing products illegal. This would have great benefit for the world, and sharply reduce profits of the leading arms-manufacturing nations (the United States, China, Britain, Israel, and rogue armament countries).[2] This process has begun with nuclear arms, and while there are many problems ahead, illegal shipping of nuclear arms appears to be diminishing dramatically.

However, any arms ban would not work unless there were security guarantees for those states afraid of aggression. That is, states import arms because they are afraid of enemies within the nation and outside of it (and use this fear to hold on to and extend their power). Also, the military elite in all states becomes accustomed to living in a shopping plaza with endless goodies. Global disincentives would be needed as well.

A world governing structure that could provide security through a type of insurance plan or through a global police system may help to reduce the demand for global weapons. The supply option would require big states to end their addiction to easy money. "Every year the most powerful nations of the world spend over $1,000 billion in weapons. The dollars saved could be spent on forming peace activist forces trained in mediation and peacekeeping skills."[3]

Transformation must occur most urgently in the global economy. Poverty, and more accurately relative deprivation— knowing that others just as talented as you and your society are doing better financially because of unfair advantages—are among the deeper causes of conflict and war. We must create a Glocalization Movement to help end poverty and see to it that wealth circulates with more justice than at present. Glocalization tries to keep the benefits of globalization (freer movement of ideas, capital, and people) along with the benefits of the local (keeping money circulating in your own area; ensuring that there is also distribution while there is growth).[4]

## WORLDVIEW

Dimensions of society other than the military-industrial complex also need transformation, particularly our worldview. At present, it helps create the conditions for war. Moments of national military trauma become part of our identity creation. War creates a national consciousness: We know who we are through battles with others. Whether it is the Star Spangled Banner and the victory of the Americans over the British, or the defeat of Serbs in Kosovo, war defines who we are.[5]

But this is not the only form of possible self-identification. We can define ourselves differently. A planetary project—whether transforming global warming or creating a global governing system or ending poverty or even space exploration—seems more likely to help us find deeper reasons for being than warfare. We also need peace education that celebrates *ahimsa* (the doctrine of not harming any living being), that celebrates moments of transcendence, that teaches us how to mediate conflict, and that celebrates the challenges humanity has faced (not any particular tribe within it) and will continue to face.[6]

## GROUP CONSCIOUSNESS

Underneath this system of war—the war industry, education, and economy—is a defining group consciousness, a deeper culture. It has a variety of pillars, three of which are most important. Challenging the idea of war as *natural* means challenging these three pillars (life is about domination, life is about survival of the fittest, and life is about ego-identity).

The first pillar is *patriarchy*, or dominator-oriented politics. Truth, nature, and reality are defined in dominator terms and not in partnership terms. What matters most is who is above and who is below. We see the world in terms of feeling superior or feeling inferior. Cultures are seen as evolved or primitive, civilized or barbaric.

Second, evolution is seen as *survival of the fittest*, and thus war is seen as just, because the fittest have survived, instead of as an evolutionary failure. Victory thus justifies evolution.

However, as biologist Lynn Margulis and evolutionary biologist Elisabeth Sahtouris argue, it is cooperation among bacteria that has led to our evolutionary development. Cooperation at all levels maximizes our survival and thrival possibilities.[7]

Third, identity is defined in terms of *ego attachment* to land, race, and language. Thus identity is seen in terms of geo-sentiment (my land, love it or leave it!), race (my color is superior), or linguistic politics, and not in more universal terms. Religion is seen as exclusionary, for the chosen few, or for those with special access to the transcendental, and not for all. While this may have been necessary in tribal politics to identify "stranger danger," there are no reasons for this today at the global level.

How can these views be challenged? First, by asserting that cooperation can lead to mutual learning.[8] Second, by asserting that evolution is not merely about survival of the fittest but involves three additional aspects: an attraction to the sublime, even spiritual; an ability to be guided through human reason and action; and an ability to become ethical. And finally, by asserting that we can develop a planetary *Gaian* consciousness. A *Gaian* consciousness sees the planet as living. We live in symbiotic relationship to our hosts and need to nurture the planet, as she nurtures us. We *can* create our destiny.[9]

### INNER AND OUTER, INDIVIDUAL AND SOCIETY
Along with our four levels of analysis, we can analyze the futures of war with a simple two-by-two table. On one axis is inner to outer, and on the other axis is individual and collective. From this table, different types of strategies emerge. The challenge is to engage at *all* levels: an individual's inner self (meanings); an individual's outer self (behaviors); society's inner self (myths and collective unconscious); and society's collective outer (structures and institutions).

|  | Inner | Outer |
|---|---|---|
| **Self** | Developing inner peace | Thinking Glo-cally and acting Glo-cally |
|  | Universal spiritual practices | Not supporting companies that engage in the war industry |
|  | Creating a balanced self | Starting peace businesses |
|  | Being the change I want to see |  |
| **Collective** | Moving away from the dominator view to the cooperative model of evolution | Glo-calization |
|  | New metaphors and symbols for peace and war | Rewriting of history textbooks |
|  | Challenging unconscious fears from prehistoric tribal eras—fear of the other | Movies about humanity's challenges |
|  |  | Creating global governance |
|  |  | New planetary project |

Using this type of analysis, there are many activities and strategies we can engage in, and most important, begin to imagine and create a world without war.

### TRANSFORMING THE FIELD

Before the war on Saddam Hussein and Iraq, Robert Muller, a former UN assistant secretary general, commented that he was not depressed at what might happen, since millions were in fact waging peace.[10]

Yes, it was unlikely that President George W. Bush and Saddam Hussein were capable of a peaceful and just resolution, but their worldviews had motivated millions to express frustration, and to call for, indeed, meme a new world. Memes are like genes but focused on ideas. Memes are ideas that pass from person to person, and become selected because they offer us advantages in our thinking, in our survival and thrival. Certainly, war as a meme, I would argue, has reached its limits in terms of offering longer-lasting solutions to Earth's problems.

Another world is possible! We need a field that begins the process of moving beyond the world of hawks and doves, and a world that recognizes that multiple traditions are required to transform war and peace. Within our histories are resources of peace, whether Islamic, Vedic, Christian, Buddhist, or secular.

But first we must challenge the litany of war. Unless it is contested, we will assume that because it *is*, it always will be. The next task is to challenge the systems that support war: the military-industrial export complex; national education systems; and our historical identities. We also need to challenge the worldviews that support and are perpetuated by war: patriarchy and survival of the fittest. Ultimately, we need a new story of what it means to be human.

**AND NEXT?**

What then are the alternative futures of warfare? Four stand out as plausible possibilities and seriously challenge us. First, **war now and forever**. We cannot transform war because humans are violent and greedy for land, territory, and ideas. Witness history. Whether it is capitalists ruling, or prime ministers and priests or warriors and kings, or workers revolting, war is the result and is used by each social class to maintain its power.

The nature of war changes depending on which social class is in power (worker, warrior, intellectual, or capitalist), and it also changes depending on the nature of technology. Most recently, air power with real-time surveillance has dominated. Nanotechnology will probably expand humanity's capacity to become both more destructive and more precisely targeted. The capacity of one leader to hold a population hostage, as with Slobodan Milosevic, Pol Pot, and Saddam Hussein, is likely to decrease dramatically. However, at the same time, the capacity of any person to hold a nation hostage will increase.

Second, **war becomes ritualized or contained**. Generally, in this future scenario, we move to a peace culture but periods of war remain. However, these are rapidly contained or conducted with the authority of a global governing system. War remains an option, even if a less desirable one. Additionally, war is used by those challenging the world governing system and by areas not totally integrated by the world system. War could even become ritualized, either conducted through virtual means or via sports. In such ways, aggression is contained and channeled.

Third, **war itself changes**. Genetic engineering and other invasive technological procedures search for the "aggression gene" with the hope of eliminating the behavior that leads to war. Some states, however, reserve the right to manipulate the "aggression" gene to make even fiercer fighters. Deeper efforts to transform systems of war are not tried, as nations are unwilling to let go of their war-industry profits. Efforts to tame war wind up maintaining the status quo.

Last and most idealistic among the four possibilities, **war disappears**. It does so because of changes in the system of war (the military-industrial complex), in the worldview that supports war (patriarchy, capitalism, and identity politics), and in the nature of what it means to be human. We take an evolutionary step toward full humanness. Proponents note that we have had periods in history without war. Moreover, humans have begun to imagine a world without war.[11]

### TAKE YOUR CHOICE

Which of these futures is most likely? Historical experience suggests the first scenario—*war now and forever*. However, the future informed by new readings of evolutionary theory maintains that *war disappears* is also possible. At the same time, because new ideas are often taken over by structures of power and those in power, we should not be surprised by the *containment of war* scenario or even the *geneticization of war*. In short, all four options must be taken seriously.

What then, as creative shapers of a more desirable future, should we do?: Remain idealistic about creating a future *without* war and act across life to achieve it. Work on achieving peace *within*. Use mediation and conflict resolution in all of our institutions. And never stop participating in the wider struggle against social systems and worldviews that help create wars.

## NOTES

1  Fred Polak, *The Image of the Future* (Amsterdam: Elsevier Scientific Publishing Company, 1973), 137–138.

2  However, given current economic dependence on arms export (as with tobacco exports), nations should be given a decade or decades to overcome their addiction to easy arms money. Of course, there would still be illegal arms smuggling but at least the large states would not be condoning it. Certainly, realizing this will not be easy. It would require international treaties that could be verified. But why might this occur? As with other regulations, pressure from lobby groups, social movements, and nongovernmental organizations might lead to new arms sales regulations. Also, a global change is possible if a player wants an advantage, that is, because of too many arms dealers, a particular player like the United States intervenes to regulate the market so that it can enhance its own trading at the expense of others. It also may be realized in a step-by-step fashion, that is, certain arms are banned—land mines—as a first step, and then slowly, other arms.

As well as sticks, there are carrots in the emerging peace business. Peace business is based on the ideas of Johan Galtung and Jack Santa-Barbara, Ph.D. Santa-Barbara trained as an experimental social psychologist, founded a company that became the largest of its kind in Canada, and won the "50 Best Privately Managed Companies" award in 1997. He has founded a new institute to promote integration of ecological and economic goals in government decision making.

http://www.humanities.mcmaster.ca/~mpeia/projectteam2.html.

3  Julio Godoy, "Political Obstacles Slow Path to Goals," Other
   News—IPS: http://www.ipsnews.net/interna.asp?idnews=22444.

4  Sohail Inayatullah, theme editor, "Global Transformations and
   World Futures," *UNESCO Encyclopedia of Life Support Systems*
   (Oxford, U.K.: EOLSS Publishers, 2002).

5  Hoping for an invasion from Mars as in *Mars Attacks* and endless
   other movies only continues to create an us vs. them mentality.

6  We need to rewrite textbooks in nearly every nation and move
   away from the Great Man or Dynastic theory of macrohistory.
   Creating alternative futures not only requires a rethinking and
   reacting of the present but a recovery of our lost and alternative
   histories. Just as there are many futures ahead of us, there are
   different histories to explore. This includes exploring history
   from other perspectives like that of a worker, the wife or mother
   of a killed warrior, a tree, ice, or other cultures, as well as
   exploring technology histories like that of the toilet. What we
   think and write about repeats the paths trodden in history, and
   thus, creates the paths we are likely to travel in the future. The
   work of Riane Eisler is exemplary: www.partnershipway.org.
   Also, see Johan Galtung and Sohail Inayatullah, eds., *Macrohistory and Macrohistorians* (Westport, Conn.: Praeger, 1997).

7  David Loye's alternative reading of Darwin is crucial here. See
   David Loye, *Darwin's Lost Theory of Love* (San Jose, Calif.: iUni-
   verse.com, 2000). Also, see David Loye, ed., *The Great Adventure*
   (New York: State University of New York Press, 2004).
   http://www.edge.org/documents/ThirdCulture/n-Ch.7.html.
   Elisabeth Sahtouris, *Earth Dance: Living Systems in Evolution*
   (San Jose, Calif.: iUniverse.com, 2002).

8  This remains among the lasting messages of the *Star Trek* series,
   especially in its latest incarnations.

9  This worldview transformation involves a change in two main
   symbols we use as a metaphor for war—the hawk and the dove.
   Can there be a third space, another story that can represent a
   world without war but with justice? Coming up with a new
   metaphor will not solve the issue, but our failure to do so highlights our conceptual problems. Perhaps looking for stories in
   our evolutionary past is not the way to go. Creating a postwar
   world may mean looking to the future for ways out.

10  www.westbynorthwest.org/artman/publish/printer_340.shtml.
    Article by Lynee Twist, 14 March 2003.
11  To create the new means being able to first conceptualize it.
    Next comes finding ways to make the impossible possible. The
    last stage is merely one of details. The details in this case are
    about creating a culture of meditation and of conflict resolution.
    This means making it central in schooling at one level, and
    beginning to create the process of global-local governance,
    where war becomes impossible.

 *  For more on Sarkar, see Sohail Inayatullah, *Understanding
    Sarkar: The Indian Episteme, Macrohistory and Transformative
    Knowledge* (Leiden, Netherlands: Brill, 2002).

## ■ Essay Sixteen ■

# PEACEMAKING: FROM TALK TO ACTION

Robert J. Merikangas, Ph.D.
Adjunct Professor, University of Maryland

Yes, let's never lose sight of our *overarching* goal—the securing soon of world peace and general well-being. We need to take action, but we need to talk before, during, and afterward, because we need to reach agreement on our agendas. While there is nothing wrong with our random acts of kindness, they are just not enough.

We cannot leave talking to the ruling elites and their diplomats, admirals, and generals because we need to imagine steps to a peaceful and bountiful world that lies outside their mental maps. They are unable to lead us there from here; *we* have to do the leading. We need to talk, then, from where we are now—on the margins and on the periphery—and then move our conversations into the halls of power.[1]

### MATTERS TO EXPLORE

To begin with, there is the mind-boggling size of the military budget. We need to talk about what President Dwight D. Eisenhower warned us about, the military-industrial complex, and what has come to be known since Eisenhower as the permanent war economy. We could use data from the Center for Defense Information and other resources outside the Pentagon to help us form our own assessments and judgments. This might lead us to oppose gigantic outlays for nuclear weapons, missile-defense shields and space weapons (called Star Wars), and huge artillery weapons (Crusaders), in favor of funding for peacemaking and peacekeeping organizations and interventions.

Second, we will mull the foundations of people's judgments about the ethics of killing. We have centuries of complex legal codes, specifying when killing another person is permissible and when it is not. There are rules of war: who may be killed and when, and with what kinds of weapons. We recognize the rights of military personnel to refuse orders to carry out killings that are not right. What do we think of these rules? What about the U.S. rule against assassination of a foreign leader?

Third, we should ask representatives of religions whether and how they justify killing by members of their faiths. We may inquire into the genocide committed by Christians in Rwanda and the reluctance of other Christians to intervene. Islamic scholars have provided interpretations of the messages of peace in their tradition, and some have criticized sponsors of terrorism and suicide bombings.

What could have a tremendous impact is a growing interpretation of the death of Jesus on the cross as a sign of non-retaliatory nonviolence, intended as the model for all his followers. (The debates about the film *The Passion of the Christ*, released in February 2004, raised many issues about the crucifixion and Christian attitudes toward Jews, Romans, and the use of violence in general.) A refusal to respond to violence with violence would be a sea change in a Christian religion in which leaders have often justified military violence, notably in the Crusades. Non-retaliation may be seen as a fundamental grounding of all universal human rights programs and campaigns.

We need to talk about what Chris Gray calls *Postmodern War*. He points out: "Some say war can never be abolished, but the same was said about slavery. It too was a very old discourse, and yet now it is almost totally discredited. Abolition of war is possible."[2] We can refuse to participate in it, as have many in Eastern Europe, the Philippines, and South Africa. Suppose they gave a war and nobody came?

(Of course, antiwar warriors will have to risk their lives as do soldiers. Gray notes this situation: "Many peace activists around the world, even in Western countries, have had friends murdered by the state; they have seen people killed; they have been chased by cars, trucks, police, soldiers; and they have been captured, beaten, and locked up. These nonviolent activists have seen more violence than most military people.")[3]

Finally, we need to wrestle with the issue in governance. For a number of years, even decades, many observers and scholars have seen that the necessary next stage in world history is the move to a system of international governance, taking the formation of the United Nations as the first step, and moving beyond to a more complete system. In a new global system, order would be kept by an international police force, not as in the past, by military campaigns of nation-states and empires, such as the British Empire.[4]

To get to this next stage, citizens everywhere need to move faster than their governments, and reach transnational agreements on a cosmopolitan or world citizenship and a corresponding higher loyalty for everyone. One way to imagine this move is to learn from the experiences of civil servants of international organizations, like the UN.

**INSTITUTE OF PEACE**

As advocates of peace-building moves, we could work with the U.S. Institute of Peace, which since its founding in 1984, has done its best with little funding and far too little visibility. America's high schools, in particular, could go out of their way to have students participate in the institute's annual National Peace Essay Contest.[5]

Each state winner is awarded a $1,000 scholarship to fund college studies and an all-expenses-paid trip to Washington, D.C., to participate in a special June awards program. Each state winner also qualifies for a chance to compete for the first-place national scholarship award of $10,000, as well as second- and third-place scholarships of $5,000 and $2,500, respectively.

**THE ARMY'S PEACEKEEPING INSTITUTE**

Another resource, the Army War College's Peacekeeping

Institute in Carlisle, Pennsylvania, has operated quietly and earnestly, if also out of the public eye, for many years.

A measure of how vital many in the public (and probably also in the military) think the institute's work is was provided when news unexpectedly broke that it was scheduled to be shut down in 2003. Protest was immediate:

> Is Donald Rumsfeld afraid to give peace a chance? Academically, at least, it appears the answer is yes. The Army War College's Peacekeeping Insitute in Carlisle, Pa., the only government entity dedicated to the task, will close by summer's end, even while the military struggles to keep the peace in Iraq. Army officials say the closure, endorsed by Rumsfeld, is a money-saving measure, though the institute's $1 million annual budget represents only .00025% of the military's annual $400 billion outlay.[6]

Thanks in large part to the outcry, the plans were put on hold. Eventually it was decided to keep the institute going, under the new name of U.S. Army Peacekeeping and Stability Operations Institute.

**K–12 PEACE STUDIES**
Peace education cannot begin soon enough, if peace is to have a chance. All the better, therefore, is the dedication of many public and private schools in addressing related matters, like the problem of bullies. These schools use creative and caring programs that make it possible for children of any age to learn how to talk about solutions (planned conflict resolution and mediation training) in place of taunting and fighting.

More and more classroom time and effort could go into helping students improve their skills and techniques for dealing with difficult and often dangerous situations where differences of opinion are seemingly deadlocked. They could practice nonviolent conflict resolution, along with the use of mediation, instead of "dissing" one another or fighting. Participation could be encouraged in Quaker programs in Alternatives to

Violence training and its youth program, HIP (Helping Increase the Peace).

Quite a few study resources these days help middle and high school students learn how to debate, how to "take sides" in a nonviolent confrontation. Drawing on a variety of political, cultural, and philosophical insights, these textbooks provide students and general readers with vital information about non-violence in theory and practice while encouraging them to evaluate critically the arguments for and against nonviolence.[7]

Finally, schools could give credit for projects of pro-peace student organizations related to community service, political advocacy, and experiential learning. Typical projects might involve successful participation in work camps, home visits, or peace camps that try to bring together people who traditionally do not get along. In all, students could be encouraged to add peace education to their personal portfolios (for use later in seeking college admission or employment).

## DEPARTMENT OF PEACE

To move out now beyond what is immediately available to a vision of a *preferred* future, and to share a scenario for making significant progress, we have a major option we could champion that has been promoted for more than twenty years.

Our country has a Cabinet-level Department of Defense (originally, a Department of War). Why not also a Cabinet-level *Department of Peace*? Drawing on ideas advanced in the 1970s, a basic framework was proposed by Congressman Dennis Kucinich of Ohio before and during his presidential campaign in 2003–2004:

1) The first day of each year, January 1, could be designated as Peace Day. All of us would be encouraged to celebrate the blessings of peace and pledge to promote peace in the coming year.

2) We could also establish a department in the executive branch of the federal government dedicated to peace-making and the study of conditions that are conducive

to domestic and international peace. It would be headed by a Secretary of Peace, appointed by the president with the advice and consent of the Senate.

Our new Department of Peace—perhaps the first such unit anywhere in the world—would promote justice and democratic principles to expand human rights; strengthen nonmilitary means of peacemaking; promote the development of human potential; work to create peace, prevent violence, and divert parties from armed conflict; and develop new structures in nonviolent dispute resolution.

The department would take a proactive, strategic approach in the development of policies that promote national and international conflict prevention, nonviolent intervention, mediation, peaceful resolution of conflict, and structured mediation of conflict.[8]

## PEACE ACADEMY

To buttress all of this, the new department would establish a Peace Academy, modeled after the military service academies (West Point, the Naval Academy), which would provide a four-year diploma-degree concentration program in peace education. Graduates would be required to serve five years in public service in programs dedicated to domestic or international nonviolent conflict resolution.[9]

## CLOSING CHALLENGES

At present we have no Peace Academy, and we make no systematic use of peace studies.[10] Little wonder we floundered so badly and at such a high cost in lives and suffering in postwar Iraq. How are we to become far more effective quickly in peacemaking and peacekeeping? And, how can you help deter war and promote peace?

NOTES

1 Our conversations could take place first, in people's study circles, in every school, and every community. We can use as a model the study circles in Sweden (Oliver 1987) and some in operation in the United States. (see the Study Circles Web site—http://www.studycircles.com/—and Linda Stout's Spirit in Action initiative). We can provide resources for our conversations on the Web, along with training materials for our facilitators. Our study circles could create regional and national networks, and make videos for use on the mass media.

2 Chris Hables Gray, *Postmodern War: The New Politics of Conflict* (New York: Guilford Press, 1997), 252.

3 *Ibid.*, 240.

4 While awaiting a humane and democratic system of world governance, a major question is that of the legitimacy of humanitarian intervention. The U.S. invasion of Iraq in 2003 is now being represented by our government as an act of humanitarian intervention rather than a defensive war against an imminent threat of attack, because no weapons of mass destruction or delivery systems were found (as of November 2004). Unauthorized humanitarian intervention is that which has not been approved by the United Nations Security Council under Chapter VII of the Charter (as in the case of NATO's military actions in Kosovo).

5 www.usip.org/ed/npec/.

6 Mark Thompson, "The Price of Peacekeeping? Too High," *Time*, 7 July 2003, 18.

7 One especially good text offers the following: Assuming the role of jurors in a simulated trial in which nonviolence must prove its effectiveness, readers will be asked to listen attentively and impartially to the first-person testimonies given by expert witnesses for the prosecution (the realists) and for the defense (the idealists). Jurors will weigh direct and circumstantial evidence; rethink their preconceived opinions; follow up on possible questions for cross-examination; explore further readings; consider exhibits such as illustrations, films, and Web sites; and, finally, find nonviolence guilty or not guilty as charged by the realists (Steger, xv).

8  See http://www.house.gov/kucinich/action/peace_legis_summary.htm.

9  The idea for a Peace Academy is not new. Some of us worked for it more than twenty years ago, and peace studies programs have been instituted in some public and private universities over the years. Such an academy was recommended by a commission, chaired by Senator Spark Matsunaga (D-Hawaii), which delivered a powerful report, "To Establish the United States Academy of Peace" (1981). The Academy of Peace did not happen, though eventually the U.S. Institute of Peace was established.

10  A masterful report on "Preventing Deadly Conflict" was made available in free copies and on the Web in 1997. The Carnegie Commission on Preventing Deadly Conflict used a public health model, and outlined operational and structural strategies for leaders of governments and organizations. We have no excuse if we have not talked about it and moved to the actions it recommends.

## REFERENCES

Caplan, Bryan. "The Literature of Nonviolent Resistance and Civilian-Based Defense" (from *Humane Studies Review*, 9:1). www.theihs.org/libertyguide/hsr/hsr.php/25.html. Accessed 15 January 2004.

Carnegie Commission on Preventing Deadly Conflict. "Preventing Deadly Conflict. Final Report with Executive Summary." New York: Carnegie Corporation of New York, 1997. www.ccpdc.org.

Department of Peace proposal: www.house.gov/kucinich/action/peace.htm.

Gray, Chris Hables. *Postmodern War: The New Politics of Conflict.* New York: Guilford Press, 1997.

Holzgrefe, J.L., and Robert O. Keohane, eds. *Humanitarian Intervention: Ethical, Legal, and Political Dilemmas.* New York: Cambridge University Press, 2003.

McCarthy, Colman. *I'd Rather Teach Peace.* Maryknoll, N.Y.: Orbis Books, 2002.

Oliver, Leonard P. *Study Circles: Coming Together for Personal Growth and Social Change*. Washington, D.C.: Seven Locks Press, 1987.

Paley, Vivian Gussin. *You Can't Say You Can't Play*. Cambridge, Mass.: Harvard University Press, 1992.

Steger, Manfred B. *Judging Nonviolence: The Dispute between Realists and Idealists*. New York: Routledge, 2003.

Stout, Linda. www.spiritinaction.net

Study Circles: www.studycircles.org

"To Establish the United States Academy of Peace: Report of the Commission on Proposals for the National Academy of Peace and Conflict Resolution to the President of the United States and the Senate and House of Representatives of the United States Congress." Washington, D.C.: Government Printing Office, 1981.

# Epilogue

## ON USING FUTURISTICS

*Where there is no vision, the people perish.*
—Proverbs 29:18,
King James Version

Where making a finer future is concerned, we have a lot going for us. To take just four revealing examples from hundreds: In 2002, three out of five college students volunteered in direct service work helping others, and within that group nearly 90 percent had volunteered in high school as well.[1] The number of firms owned by women is rising at twice the rate of all businesses; the number of minority-owned businesses is growing four times faster than the national rate.[2] Federal welfare rolls continue to decline, and the number of welfare families in 2004 was less than half when the law was changed in 1996.[3] Life expectancy, a summary sort of measure of 101 subsidiary matters, has gone from 47 years in 1900 to 73 for males and 79 for females, and is likely to climb into the mid-80s by 2020.[4] In all, an encouraging picture.

Given these improvements, it is not surprising—albeit very welcome—to learn that by one informed estimate, as many as one in three Americans worries about the environment; works to improve their communities; wants products to be made in a sustainable way; spends to promote good health and personal development; and never stops trying to translate constructive values into effective and lasting action.[5]

This is not to deny our many persistent national problems—including runaway health care costs. (43 million Americans, one in six, live without health insurance).[6] Almost 12 million children still live under the federal poverty line (along with

175

more than 23 million adults).[7] Overworked parents have twenty-two fewer hours per week than in 1969 to spend with their children.[8] Millions of employees worry about whether their jobs are staying on our shores. Only 17 percent of young Americans voted in 2002 versus 39 percent of all eligible Americans.[9] Far too many recent retirees rely on only their Social Security checks. Close to a million people suffer from AIDS. Everyone quietly fears another 9/11, although this time as a chemical or nuclear nightmare. And as for life expectancy, while we led the world fifty years ago, most recently American women ranked only twentieth and men only twenty-second among advanced industrial nations.[10]

Not to gainsay any of our challenges, but the good news serves to help us understand why the United States remains the most desired destination for immigrants from around the planet. They know that we continue to make progress in realizing the American Dream, one they envy. Our problems, while deep-set and long-standing, are *not* intractable, and are not protected by fundamentalism or strangling traditions. We steadily gain on our challenges.

Better yet, we have reason to expect fresh help from two commonly overlooked sources, namely, the polar ends of the age continuum, our youngsters and our grandparents. Our children, now in the lower grades, as "in any society in crisis, [are] the first to learn to incorporate the worst of threats into the most basic forms of play ... [they possess] the leaps of consciousness that will be required for us to navigate our paths."[11] Similarly, "it may be the old ... whose wisdom has the most to offer ... [they can help] restore caring and sharing to their proper place in human history."[12]

If we choose to take heart from progress under way, lose sleep over how much always remains to be accomplished, listen anew to the children and our elders, we can together move America steadily along. In our final essay we are reminded how much we can rapidly accomplish and we are nudged, encouraged, and inspired to do so.—Editor

176

1 Ganesh Sitaraman and Previn Warren, "Why Young Americans Hate Politics," in Andrew Cuomo, ed., *Crossroads: The Future of American Politics* (New York: Random House, 2003), 254–55.

2 Ad, "Found Money," Microsoft, *New York Times*, 25 March 2004, A27.

3 Robert Pear, "Despite Sluggish Economy, Welfare Rolls Actually Fell," *New York Times*, 22 March 2004, A21.

4 DeWitt Publishing, "Paving the Way toward New Cures," *New York Times*, 22 March 2004, C14.

5 Amy Cortese, "They Care about the World and They Shop, Too," *New York Times*, 20 July 2003, 4BU.

6 Dennis Rivera, "America Is Hurting," in Andrew Cuomo, ed., *Crossroads, op. cit.*, 231.

7 Russell Simmons, "Ending Poverty and Ignorance: Transforming American Society from the Perspective of the Hip-Hop Generation," in *Ibid.*, 248.

8 Senator John Edwards, "Building a Nation as Strong as Its Spirit," in *Ibid.*, 105.

9 Sitaraman and Warren, "Why Young Americans Hate Politics," in *Ibid.*, 254.

10 Rivers, *op. cit.*

11 Douglas Rushkoff, *Playing the Future: How Kids' Culture Can Teach Us to Thrive in an Age of Chaos* (New York: HarperCollins, 1996), 8, 11.

12 Theodore Roszak, *America the Wise: The Longevity Revolution and the True Wealth of Nations* (Boston, Mass.: Houghton Mifflin, 1998), 248. Note also that since 2000 those over sixty-five have been "the fastest-growing group to embrace the online world." Katie Hafner, "For Some Internet Users, It's Better Late than Never," *New York Times*, 25 March 2004, G1.

## ■ Essay Seventeen ■

# CREATING YOUR OWN FUTURE: YOU ARE ONLY THIRTY SECONDS AWAY

### Roger Kaufman, Ph.D.
Director, Roger Kaufman & Associates

Thirty seconds? You've got to be kidding!

No, thirty seconds is all it takes for you to be the master of change, not the victim of change. Decide now to take control and create your future, not drift into it.

Certainly, things don't always appear under control. People you know often seem stressed, distracted, and to be doing destructive things. And there is a lot of pressure from friends to "go along." Pressures and problems seem to surround us at times.

But that is only *What Is* and not necessarily *What Should Be* or *What Could Be.*

I have some ideas to share that may help you create a bit more happiness—ideas that are simple and can put you in control of more of your life. And from this you are in a better position to build a future you really want.

But the thirty seconds? What's that about? Two great psychotherapists—Harold Greenwald and Theodore Blau—agree that it only takes thirty seconds to decide to change your life. The tough part is getting ready to make that decision.

There are two major parts to creating your own future: first, getting ready to *define* the kind of world in which you want to live. And second, deciding to change to deliver that to yourself.

Take a look into your future. What are you doing now to make that a better future? What are you doing now that will make it a poor future?

To help get started, here are seven guidelines to consider:

1) *A fact doesn't cease to exist simply because you choose to ignore it.* If we don't kid ourselves, grim aspects of reality are all around us. We see war, poverty, drugs, malnutrition, sickness, and these are not good for our health and well-being—not good for anyone.

    We see people around us encouraging us and others to do things we know are destructive (but perhaps fun, at first) and we know are not smart. Facts are facts. Don't kid yourself, and don't sell your soul for a few minutes of acceptance. It is *your* future, not theirs.

2) *We are what we do.* Talk is cheap. We are what we do. And whatever we do requires us to be responsible for the consequences. We control much of our future. Do what is useful.

    We see people who want to create and maintain peace, and help others become self-sufficient and healthy. We see still others who are willing to provide us with the tools (like a decent education) and resources to make our world better. Try learning from them and taking their example to heart. Why are you in school? Just to pass the time until you can get out, or to pick up some useful knowledge for your future?

3) *Move out of your comfort zone—today's paradigms and ways of thinking and acting—and use new and wider boundaries for what you plan and do.* Want to be happy and successful? You have to decide to be happy, and that often means taking the risk of changing how you act and what you do now. The riskiest thing is to do the same thing over and over again and expect different results.

4) *Differentiate between ends (what) and means (how). Prepare all objectives to measure accomplishment.* This seems silly at first, but it is very important. Most people jump right into solutions (skip an appointment, take easy courses, hang out with cool kids, do what others do) before knowing the ends they want (self-respect, health, happiness, creation of a future that is safe and

satisfying). Pick your solutions only on the basis of the
results and payoffs you really want; select your means
on the basis of desired ends.

5) *Use a worldview—an Ideal Vision of what kind of world, in
   measurable performance terms, we want for all of us,
   including tomorrow's child, as the underlying basis for planning, decision making, and continuous improvement.*
   Think in terms of how you can add value to our
   shared world. You already do a lot in this area if you
   recycle, if you don't jeopardize yourself and others
   (don't pour that used motor oil in the drain), and do
   everything to make our world and yours better.

6) *Use all three levels of planning and results: one for our
   immediate actions, one for the results for our family and
   friends, and a third for our shared society.* Link what we
   use, do, produce, and deliver to add value outside of
   ourselves and others, to all stakeholders. Ask each time
   you make a decision: Will this take me closer or further away from adding value to society?

7) *Define "need" as a gap in results (not as insufficient levels
   of resources, means, or methods). Needs* are gaps in results;
   gaps in ends and payoffs. Make sure you know the
   gaps in results before you pick ways and means of
   doing things. For example, instead of saying "I *need* a
   new BMW," look at the gaps in results in terms of
   safety and convenience for getting from here to there.

So there you are, seven guides for making useful decisions
and creating your future. You decide.

Thirty seconds. Let's look at that a bit closer in terms of
what goes into your decision to create your own future. Getting ready for that most important thirty seconds is based on
seven practical steps listed below. Let's take a closer look:

1) What payoffs or consequences (like feeling blue,
   rejected, or overweight) are you getting now that you
   don't want? Please list them.

2)  What are the behaviors that you do that deliver these negative payoffs? Please list them.

3)  What payoffs do you want? Please list them.

4)  Identify the behaviors that will deliver the payoffs you want. Please list them.

5)  Decide to change from your current behaviors to the ones that will deliver the positive payoffs you want. Go ahead, decide. THIS IS THE CRITICAL THIRTY SECONDS!

6)  Begin to change your behaviors—yes, resolve to really change how you behave and act.

7)  Be ready to decide to change over and again in the future when you want *new and different* payoffs.

Your decision to use the seven guides and seven steps for helping to create a finer future is doable.

Want to work at creating a better, happier, and more successful future? These are the essentials. Much of your future remains up to you—and I am betting on you.

APPENDIX

Here are some statements you can think about that can help you decide if you want to change:

### Statements to Consider

| Always | Frequently | Sometimes | Not Usually | Never |
| --- | --- | --- | --- | --- |

What I do now makes a difference to me in five years.

My parents are wrong.

What others are doing now doesn't hurt anyone.

What I do with my life can make a difference in the world.

Teachers are wrong.

Adults don't understand young people.

I can make a difference for myself.

I can make a difference for others.

What I do is harmless.

Courtesy of The Venus Project
Designed by Jacque Fresco and Roxanne Meadows

# Appendix

## STUDENT FEEDBACK

Sixteen high school volunteers read more than sixty candidate essays and offered feedback on many (though not on all) that influenced the final selection. Their (anonymous) views below are listed in the order in which they arrived back to me. They join me in hoping this material helps you take more from the essays.

**FUTURE JOB TRENDS: PUZZLES, PITFALLS, AND PRIZES**
*—JIM PINTO*

1) I really enjoyed this essay. The "near-term" and "long-term" effects are something that I really liked. With such widespread use of technology today, this essay provides an interesting insight into where technology will be in the *future*.

**INNOVATING THE FUTURE—*ANN COOMBS***
*WITH MALCOLM MORGAN*

1) I like this essay, but I do not know if regular teens would. It might be a little too radical for them. Many teens might not find it easy or even realistic to go against the norm. Kids are really concerned about their image and do not want to be the odd one out. However, at the end of the essay, I do like the quiz. That kind of shows the reader that you do not really have to be that radical. It shows that there are different degrees of being an innovator.

2) I would reject this one. It feels like one of those "spam" surveys you would get from a fraudulent e-mail server. There really is not much of a message, at least not one that teenagers are not presented with every day by teachers, parents, counselors, and countless others. As for using celebrity examples, I understand that they are relevant, but in a way it almost hurts the essay. It is just another report about the stars of our society

and what they have done (this is why my interest was already waning in the first paragraphs).

### CARE TO BE A DOCTOR TOMORROW?—*SOHAIL INAYATULLAH*

1) I love this essay. It is so interesting to see these technological advancements that I never knew were being developed. Some of the things that were said to be soon on the market are really exciting.

I do not really understand what nanotech is, though. Maybe I read it wrong, but I did not really follow what it does. I do not know how working with small atoms to create things would help kill cancer.

2) It is unclear, and we don't know much about this topic to begin with, so it is hard to make sense of this essay because it pulls the reader in many different directions.

3) This essay provides a far-reaching viewpoint on health, but it feels more like two essays instead of a single one: one explaining the different possibilities based on quotes and the second the four future paths.

Personally, I think the two parts have different styles, and I would keep the first section unchanged but perhaps condense the second so that it doesn't seem like a different essay. This then allows the list to exist and appear as part of the original essay. Overall this essay provides an interesting and definitely futuristic view of medicine, but without changing the structure of the second part, it lacks cohesion.

4) I really liked this essay. It was a little challenging to read but well written and well organized. It was a topic that I've thought about but never in such a concrete way or in so much detail. It was very comprehensive and very different from the other essays.

5) Health care is such a huge industry and so many advances have been made in the past few years that it's important to include.

6) Teens are not concerned about health care. It is way too complex for kids my age. I do not think they will find it interesting or worthwhile if they read it.

7) The essay about health care asked way too many questions in the beginning and loses the reader right off the bat. While I continued to read, I felt as if I was reading a science report or a research paper.

Although the information is interesting, I kept finding myself getting lost and having to reread it to understand it. I think the majority of teens will find this difficult to read and understand.

8) I would say use this one. In our modern world, health care has become an increasingly important issue to many people. This essay takes a good look at what is going on in the medical community and what the future holds in the industry. Many readers will find this worthwhile, although it is not really "science fiction."

### IS THERE A UNION IN YOUR FUTURE?—*DAVID REYNOLDS*

1) I thought this essay was very well written, but labor unions aren't at the top of my mind of important issues. There are so many fewer industrial workers in the United States than there were thirty years ago that this doesn't seem like a serious issue, and the government seems to protect well against exploitation.

I know what labor unions are and why they are good. But I also felt that a major issue with labor unions is that they create a somewhat socialist system, and I think in any article about labor unions that should be addressed. I thought that it was a good essay, but that it didn't really focus on different parts of the issue enough.

2) I do not like this essay. Comparing nineteenth-century unions to today is ridiculous. Government is so much more involved in regulating workplaces and no longer takes the laissez-faire attitude toward business anymore. Giving out so many benefits to workers will ruin our economy. We are a democracy. We are run by capitalism. This sounds to me an awful lot like Communism. People should get paid whatever their job allows. Giving people benefits for no reason will hurt our businesses.

3) This essay was enlightening and interesting. I liked the comparison to European countries in order to show what the United States could be like in the future if it made some changes. There was a lot of information, but the essay was succinct and provided essential information. It kept my attention all the way to the end. Definitely include it. It's a very unique concept.

4) This reads like something out of a pro-union political pamphlet. It is pretty one-sided, but you said that was what you wanted, an opinion, right? It just seems to not even mention the other side of the issue. Teens get instantly suspicious of stuff like that; it feels like advertising. Providing less background and statistics extolling unions, and more future effects would make the essay better.

5) Not having unions is what creates competition in our great capitalistic society. While they may be good for the lower-middle and working class, the rest of the workforce should not have a reason to form them. Also, receiving health care and other such benefits should depend on the employee's performance, but there also should be a national health care plan. I feel there is too much government control over industry and the economy. But the essay is well written, and it would be worth someone's time to read.

6) I found this essay on labor unions quite interesting. (A contributing factor is that my father is a labor lawyer and our typical dinner table conversation involves heated discussion about one aspect of labor unions or another.) Aside from that, this is a topic that at some point in time will affect us all; it's important for teens to be informed about labor unions and their possible transformations in the future. Also, it wasn't too long, which is nice for those who aren't extremely interested in this area.

7) I still do not agree with this essay but other kids my age might. I do not like how this essay presents one side of the issue. It does not let kids decide their stance.

## SCHOOLING IN 2010: HELPING YOUNG LEARNERS SOAR!
### —ARTHUR B. SHOSTAK

1) The idea of an Intelligent Agent is feasible and beneficial in theory but in reality, much less so. The small size of the device, which the child could easily carry, could not only be lost but broken. Trusting a child to be responsible for something that wouldn't necessarily be easy to replace is difficult.

Also, the idea of having a companion who could share knowledge with the child could have some lasting problems. One, the child has a resource at their command, dissolving the need for learning how to use the resources themselves. It takes away from the learning experience even as it makes the experience more interesting and engaging for the child.

Two, there would be potential problems with honesty. How could the teacher know if students were progressing on their own or had simply started to use the Intelligent Agent as a crutch, impeding progress?

Three, there is no substitute for an actual human companion. The thought of having a programmable companion for every child would breed antisocial tendencies (in that they wouldn't need contact with other children) and allow the child to lose touch with reality. How would they know that they were talking to a computer program/search engine with human characteristics? Potential emotional damage could occur.

## ALTERNATIVE FUTURES OF CRIME AND PRISONS
### —SOHAIL INAYATULLAH

1) This essay has a lot of innovative ideas, but it wouldn't appeal to many teenagers. It takes an interesting look at the future of crime but doesn't really relate it to young adults. I simply don't think many teens would be inclined to read this essay.

2) I would accept this essay. I have to applaud the author, who found—and subsequently wrote a very strong essay on—a topic that never would have crossed my mind in regard to the future. It is interesting to consider: If we truly are headed toward a brighter tomorrow, what is the future of crime? The

author presents interesting points and supports them with sound logic. Furthermore, many readers will find a level of comfort or satisfaction in this essay, knowing that the next generation will be better off than ours.

3) I would include this essay because it takes a look at punishment that applies to teenagers. At some point in time, almost all teens feel that they're being punished for an unnecessary reason or punished to an exaggerated extent. While this takes more of a *Law and Order* look at society as a whole instead of only as it relates to teens, it is still easy to relate it to yourself. I also liked the examples of movies—they illustrate the underlying theme better.

4) I like this essay. It is very interesting with the different ways to approach crimes in the future. By presenting all the different sides with no bias, it lets the reader decide his or her view. I like how the reader has a say. The only thing I would do to revise this essay is change the beginning. It was kind of silly and really unrealistic to go to jail for eating meat. The examples of going to jail in the future were really out there.

### JANUARY 2051: A LETTER TO MY BEST BUD IN BANGLADESH
#### —LINDA BROWN

1) To me this essay was all right. It wasn't thrilling. I do not like the idea of an essay in letter format. I do like the quiz at the end of the essay, though. I like the topic, but it is not a stunning essay. It could use a little work to become more eye-catching and enjoyable.

### FLOATING CITIES: WHERE DO YOU WANT TO LIVE TOMORROW?
#### —PATRICK G. SALSBURY

1) I didn't like this essay, but that is probably due to the fact that I think this idea is absolutely false and unthinkable. It would be wrong to study these people as if they were organisms within a petri dish.

2) A very nice essay, to which the introductory paragraphs are a good addition. The essay by itself is an interesting idea, in perhaps a direction that has not been looked at much, in either

these essays or in much of the other science fiction I've read. A good idea and a well-written piece—definitely a good candidate for inclusion.

3) I do not really like this essay. Maybe I just don't get it? I don't understand what the author is talking about (testing human beings in different environments?). It seems really far-fetched to me.

## GLOBALIZATION AND YOU—*MEDARD GABEL*

1) I really like this essay about globalization. It is fairly long, but while reading it, it didn't seem long at all. It had my attention the whole time. I like the little quiz you take in the middle of it. It grabs the attention of its readers and makes them feel a part of the essay. Globalization is an important issue in our world today. By just looking at my shoes and shirt, the message was clearly portrayed to me. Globalization has a huge effect on my life and what I wear, eat, play, etc. Other teens will be interested in this essay, too, because it is so real. This is a sure pick for the book.

2) I think this is important to include. The quiz is an eye-opener. The global economy is very important. We use other countries' products and labor, and in return, give them products or money for their labor.

3) I found this essay both humorous and interesting. It presents very accurate points, ones that have undeniable truth in our modern world. Furthermore, it calls on topics that are quite popular with my generation. The "made in China" phrase has become a favorite slogan of the next generation of Americans. All of this is presented in a humorous fashion (the globalization intensity quiz). I would accept this.

4) The essay was all right. It started out strong, but then it lost my interest. I didn't think the quiz was necessary, and the essay seemed to be repeating the same things. I liked the topic, and it's important, but I didn't like the essay.

5) This essay is an excellent choice for the book. It connects directly with students; it addresses us as equals and was very informative and interesting. I know students would like to read

this essay and would benefit from it. I really liked the quiz. It was also structured more like a person-to-person speech instead of just an informative text. I think the author does a great job connecting with his audience. You should definitely use this essay in a book.

### SHAPING TOMORROW'S FOREIGN POLICY—*CHRIS SEIPLE*

1) I liked the essay. The one part about the various alliances was a little boring, but I really liked the rest. I liked the end about what we need to do to prepare for the future and about America's future as the biggest superpower. It was different from the other essays and a lot better than the one about the future of warfare.

### FUTURE TENSE: WAR AND PEACE 2015
### —*MARILYN DUDLEY-ROWLEY AND THOMAS GANGALE*

1) I really like the format of this essay and how it was just two people talking about what they knew and agreeing and working off of what each other said. Both of them really seemed to enjoy what they were doing and have good knowledge. This is a very important topic, and one that many students really need to, and do, think about. This essay would be very beneficial for the students to read and a great selection for the book.

### FUTURE OPTIONS FOR THE MIDDLE EAST: THE ART
### OF PRACTICAL PEACEMAKING—*TSVI BISK*

1) I do not think teens will like this essay, mainly because I do not think they would understand it. I always hear about the suicide attacks on Israel and the confrontations between Israel and Islamic countries. But, despite that, I do not understand much more. I do not really understand the stance and position each side is taking. The last part about the new government in Iraq really interested me, though.

### FORECASTING IRAQ'S FUTURE: DEMOCRACY À LA ISLAM OR IS
### IT DÉJÀ VU ALL OVER AGAIN?—*USHA MENON*

1) It is a good essay, there are a lot of facts, and it is good to

show teens the different outcomes that could result in Iraq. However, I do not feel like this essay is meant for teens. It does not address them or tell them what they can do or how they may have an effect on Iraq. Maybe if the author could tell teens what the best outcome would be and what it would mean for the Middle East. And maybe the author could tell teens what they could do to help the outcome be a success.

2) I've been wondering what will happen with the government in Iraq once the troops leave. The essay presents the different possibilities well and gives good background information. It wasn't really that interesting to read, but it's an important topic, and the essay was thorough.

3) This essay is one of my favorites. I love the writing, including the statistics within the storyline in the beginning. It gives a clear idea of the situation in Iraq, which, given our country's circumstances, is a relevant and important topic. I would definitely include this in your book. It's a good read that is straight to the point and doesn't ramble.

### ALTERNATIVE FUTURES OF WAR: IMAGINING THE IMPOSSIBLE
### —SOHAIL INAYATULLAH

1) I like this essay about war. It is important to show kids my age that there is another solution to war and that war is not inevitable. This is an important issue in our chaotic world today. However, if I was the author, I would try to spice it up a little bit. Maybe the author could somehow make the essay relate to teens' lives (maybe a recent movie, violence in school).

2) I found this essay interesting, but I would not accept it for publication. Although the premise of a world without war is an interesting one, it holds little bearing for people of the modern era and would more likely than not fall on deaf ears as the people turned the page to read the next essay.

For a moment I thought the essay would be OK, when it spoke of the economic dependency on the arms trade. However, the author believes this can be overcome in a decade. This essay, needless to say, is written from an optimistic standpoint.

The author puts faith in the human ability to overcome. Realistically, war is a continual cycle.

There are too many factors—ones not addressed in this essay—that pull us apart and divide us, even though they should not: religion, ethnicity, race, natural resources, politics, and countless others. It is interesting that an essay written during our escapades into Iraq would fail to mention political gain as a motive of war.

### PEACEMAKING: FROM TALK TO ACTION
### —ROBERT J. MERIKANGAS

1) I would definitely include this essay. I not only liked the topic but the different steps and approaches it suggests for implementing peace. Especially at a time like this—during the war with Iraq and violence continuing worldwide—the essay would be educational yet entertaining for teens to read. It is straightforward and unapologetic when citing society's mistakes.

2) I thoroughly enjoyed reading this essay because it blatantly blames military institutions for our lack of worldwide peace. It is concise (not too long), and the format makes it easy to comprehend. I would definitely include it as it is a topic that affects everyone throughout the world.

3) This essay is totally '60s. I do not think teens really believe in peace. I know I don't. As much as I want there to be no war in our world, I know it is highly unlikely—especially with 9/11 and all. That day showed me that some people are so radical that nothing can stop them from inflicting pain and death on their "enemies." I think war is absolutely necessary to stop people like this from doing it again. These types of people are beyond all hope. I do not think a world without war is possible. Good and evil have always existed, and evil will always exist.

### CREATING YOUR OWN FUTURE: YOU ARE ONLY THIRTY SECONDS AWAY—ROGER KAUFMAN

1) Although teenagers might have heard the same thing

before, it never hurts to repeat this message. Many people, my age especially, have developed a pattern of life that they seem to be permanently committed to, and it is a destructive and hurtful pattern (drugs, alcohol, etc.). If this essay can change the mind-set of a couple of these people, it has already proved its worth.

2) I think teens would view this as just another essay of information they have already seen, whether in health class, or just in reading material that all teens seem to come across at some point, like *Who Moved My Cheese?* Teens would not view this as the future but rather as part of their life now. I'm not sure if it could be revised to eliminate that tone without changing the essay.

3) This essay is valuable because it is much different from the other essays. It is more personal and interactive. I think high schoolers will receive it well.

First, it asks for statements or yes or no questions. It should provide the space for the answers. It should have lines and yes's or no's to circle or fill in. This way, the readers separate their ideas from the essay, get their ideas in a permanent form and actually answer the questions. Teenagers (at least girls) are used to filling out little quizzes from popular magazines so they can relate to this easily (except this quiz will be a little more meaningful!).

4) I like this piece, and the perfect place for it is either a prologue or foreword or introduction in your book. Anything that can be done in thirty seconds will appeal to students.

Also, there are a lot of things that I would like to have, but I don't know the best approach. This article offers insight into that and other students will get the same benefit.

5) This essay is a great example of what high schoolers get a lot of all the time: cheesy, inspirational speeches that speak in vagaries and do not sink in.

High schoolers do not react well to being presented with vague self-improvement styles and that the real secret is "just deciding" to do something. This essay in particular sounds like something every kid has heard before, from parents, teachers, and counselors—everyone a kid is disinclined to listen to.

It has good strategies, but it misses the point that to a high schooler it is not as easy as "just deciding" to be or not to be a certain way. Though the author claims to understand the pressures of high school, this essay seems not to realize this point.

7) I don't like it. It's a little too didactic. It sounds like something that my Christian Lifestyles textbook might use. It was a little scattered and lengthy. The advice was very common and nothing new or interesting.

8) The very beginning is catchy, and I like how it draws its readers in immediately. Although some kids may think they're too "cool" to read this, it is very important. Teens' lives are chaotic right now, and different forces are pulling them every which way. They do not know who they are as a person yet, but they certainly have a vision of who they want to be. This essay will reassure them that this is possible. It portrays a good message to teens and tells them the importance of their future and how to control it.

9) At the beginning of this essay, I was really engaged. It appeared to me like a parody of an infomercial, which I thought was clever. It held my interest until about halfway through when I was tired of hearing about change and payoffs.

I didn't feel necessarily attacked, but I think some teens would. The essay talked about change, which is completely fine, but toward the middle it kept reinforcing the issue of change, which in some ways makes one feel inadequate—as if they're doing something very wrong. Teens are tired of hearing about how they're dysfunctional and hard to handle. Besides, I don't think this essay is really accurate.

# ABSTRACTS FROM *FUTURE SURVEY*

Michael Marien, editor

*The following abstracts were prepared by Michael Marien, founder and editor of* Future Survey, *a nonpartisan monthly newsletter published by the World Future Society since 1979. FS provides fifty abstracts every month of recent books, reports, and important articles on both global and domestic issues. FS carries items on trends, forecasts, and policy proposals on topics such as world futures, the global economy, the Middle East and other regions and nations, security, energy, the environment, governance, education, health, crime, communications, new technologies and their impacts, and methods for shaping a better future.*

## WORK/TIME POVERTY (October 2003)

*Take Back Your Time: Fighting Overwork and Time Poverty in America.* Edited by John de Graaf (Seattle, Washington; Coordinator, Take Back Your Time Day; www.timeday.org). San Francisco, Calif.: Berrett-Koehler, September 2003, 270 p.

The official handbook of Take Back Your Time Day, a new national consciousness-raising event held for the first time on October 24, 2003—nine weeks before the end of the year, to symbolize that Americans work an average of nine weeks more than our peers in Western Europe.

Chapters include: "The (Even More) Overworked American" by Juliet Schor (noting that average annual hours worked in the United States have risen from 1,703 in 1979 to 1,827 in 1995 and 1,878 in 2000); the incredible shrinking vacation for American workers; forced overtime in the land of the free (nearly one in five workers now spends more than 50 hours a week at work; 45 percent of workers have to work overtime with little or no notice); over-scheduled kids and under-connected families; the cost to civil society in less volunteer work; health hazards of overwork (our desire to keep health insurance benefits ties us to jobs that are bad for our health); the effects of time stress on pregnancy; sleep deprivation; dreams of leisure in an earlier era; lessons from the Hebrew tradition of Shabbat (by Rabbi Arthur Waskow); the time cost of American stuff (by Vicki Robin); the simplicity movement; job sharing; the growing trend toward "working retired"; the case for sabbaticals as a common feature in work life; escalating work hours creating a nursing crisis; finding the time to cook healthy food in our time-pressed lives (and the Slow Food Movement as antidote); Europe's work-time alternatives; "What's An Economy For?" by David Korten (on "the suicide economy" vs. "the living economy"); and how to organize a Take Back Your Time Day in your community.

> [NOTE: Could be the start of something big. John de Graaf is coauthor of *Affluenza: The All-Consuming Epidemic* (Berrett-Koehler, 2001; *FS* 23:6/262) and producer of PBS-TV specials on *Affluenza* and *Running Out of Time*.]

## WORK/POVERTY (October 2003)
*The Betrayal of Work: How Low-Wage Jobs Fail 30 Million Americans*. Beth Shulman (Washington D.C.; former vice president, United Food and Commercial Workers Union). New York: The New Press, September 2003, 255 p.

Old forms of poverty continue, but *"the great secret of America is that a vast new impoverished population has grown up in our midst."* These are not Americans excluded from the world of work, but the core of much of the new economy. Indeed, "our recent prosperity rests, in part, on their misery."

America's super-exploited, the invisible working poor, are both a shame and a challenge of historic proportions. They are nursing home workers, home health-care workers, poultry processors, retail store clerks, hotel and janitorial workers, call-center workers, and child-care workers—more than 30 million people who work hard every day and yet struggle to take care of their families.

Besides inadequate wages, most of these workers lack basic job benefits, and engage in work that is often physically damaging and emotionally degrading (because of constant surveillance, time clocks, drug testing, and rigid rules). The "low-skilled" label is a distancing device, allowing us to dismiss these workers as undeserving, somehow flawed.

If we honor work, we must reward it—and level the playing field for employers who are doing the right thing in providing their workers with livable wages, basic benefits, and respect. To help block the low road of degradation and to rebalance power between employers and their workers, a "Compact With Working Americans" is proposed: 1) raise the minimum wage and index it for automatic increases (the real value of today's minimum wage is 30 percent lower than in 1968); 2) require companies that receive public money to provide quality jobs; 3) emphasize full employment in monetary and fiscal policy; 4) strengthen the Earned Income Tax Credit and Child Tax Credit; 5) for part-time workers, require wage and benefit parity with full-time workers; 6) restructure work time to allow workers to care for their families; 7) provide public child-care assistance and upgrade the quality of care; and 8) strengthen whistleblower protections for a safe and healthy workplace.

For those who argue that these improvements will cost too much, "the cost of doing nothing is even greater."

[NOTE: Provides case studies of individuals, similar to the personal experiences of Barbara Ehrenreich in *Nickel and Dimed: On (Not) Getting By in America* (Owl Books, May 2002). Excellent popular companion to the industry case studies below.]

## WORK/POVERTY (October 2003)

*Low-Wage America: How Employers Are Reshaping Opportunity in the Workplace.* Eileen Appelbaum (Rutgers University), Annette Bernhardt (New York University School of Law), and Richard J. Murname (Harvard Graduate School of Education). New York: Russell Sage Foundation, September 2003, 535 p.

The most extensive study to date of how the world of work is changing for the 42 percent of American workers who have never attended college, and for workers who do not earn enough to support themselves and their families. The majority of low-wage workers in the United States have no credentials beyond a high school diploma, and many lack even this.

In 2001, about 27.5 million Americans—23.9 percent of the labor force—earned less than $8.70 an hour (which, full time for the entire year produces annual earnings of $17,400—about equal to the poverty line for a family of four, and not nearly enough to sustain most working families, e.g., two parents with two children require $27,000 to $52,000 a year to maintain a basic standard of living, depending on the community). Advances in infotech have increased economic pressures. The decline in labor unions (from 24 percent of U.S. workers in 1973 to 13 percent by 2002) has reduced the ability of workers to negotiate with managers, and all three branches of the federal government have shown greater hostility to unions in the last 20 years. Another change in the institutional environment is the decline in the real value of the minimum wage: In 1974, the minimum wage expressed in 2001 dollars was $7.18; in 2001 it was $5.15.

These case studies funded by the Future of Work Program of the Russell Sage and Rockefeller Foundations studied 464 establishments in 25 industries, interviewed 1,700 managers and workers, and compiled data from more than 10,000 surveys of workers and managers. Industries covered include hotels, hospitals, medical equipment, valve manufacturing, steel, plastics, food service, call centers, temporary employment firms, auto suppliers, and hosiery.

It concludes that "there is a clear role for government in making work pay for the many Americans who work full time in the mentally and physically demanding jobs that are the backbone of much economic activity."

The most obvious point of intervention is to raise the minimum wage. A national commitment to a living wage is needed. And enforcement of U.S. labor law is essential. Human Rights

Watch found that illegal reprisals against employees trying to form unions have risen from more than 1,000 a year in the 1950s to more than 23,000 in 1998. "The simple act of reining in this illegal activity by employers would go a long way toward re-establishing unionization as a viable choice for U.S. workers."

## BUSINESS/STOCK OPTIONS (October 2003)

*In the Company of Owners: The Truth About Stock Options—and Why You Should Have Them.* Joseph Blasi (professor of management, Rutgers University), Douglas Kruse (professor of Management, Rutgers University), and Aaron Bernstein (senior writer, *Business Week*). New York: Basic Books, January 2003, 401 p.

"The central argument of this book is that most corporations in America would enjoy more motivated workers and larger profits if they embraced partnership capitalism centered around employee stock options. This model of the corporation stimulates better economic performance through a new division of the risks and rewards of property ownership." Many technology companies came to this conclusion as their industries grew. "It seems likely that their approach will survive the tech shakeout and stand as an example in other industries."

These lessons aren't new. Traditional companies have learned at least parts of them several times over the decades. But, somehow, these ideas never seem to stick. Many corporations pursued employee ownership, but often based it on worker savings rather than true property-sharing. Many also skimped on the amounts, failing to provide workers a meaningful incentive relative to their salary. "Stock options have been thoroughly abused by most major companies, whose executives have used them to transfer ownership of more than 10 percent of the nation's corporate wealth from public shareholders to a small coterie of top officials. But companies that have offered options to their entire workforce offer a much different example."

Still, partnership capitalism may not be suitable for every company or every industry. It is likely to be more of a challenge at big companies, with a cast of thousands. And it is possible that a company can get carried away and grant too many options (some High Tech 100 employees thought that their companies sometimes overdid it). A related problem is when employees who hold options may be tempted to look for ways to artificially pump up their company's stock, even if it means cutting corners.

On the other hand, a partnership approach may offer some help in preventing options from distorting management's perspective (most rank-and-file workers would have good reason if top executives tried to cook the books, because their long-term financial interests still lie with their regular salary). Partnership capitalism also would seem to call for an employee representative to sit on the board (workers on boards have long existed in many European countries). The most important ingredient in partnership capitalism is the cultural transformation it entails, reversing the cult of the CEO that grew in the 1990s, along with enormous chasms in pay.

## WORK/U.S. LABOR LAW (October 2003)

*Workers' Rights as Human Rights.* Edited by James A. Gross (professor of labor law, School of Industrial and Labor Relations, Cornell University). Ithaca, N.Y.: ILR Press (Cornell University Press), June 2003, 272 p.

Essays arising from an October 2000 conference at Cornell University on "Human Rights in the American Workplace: Assessing U.S. Labor Law and Policy." Gross supplies background by explaining that the 1935 National Labor Relations Act (the Wagner Act) established democratic procedures for participation of workers in determining their wages, hours, and working conditions. Although not using the term *human rights*, "the Wagner Act was far ahead of its time in applying human rights principles to U.S. workplaces."

But the 1947 Taft-Hartley amendments to the Wagner Act

legitimized employer opposition to the organization of employees. U.S. labor law has failed, despite the assertion of the 1948 Universal Declaration of Human Rights that everyone has the right to form and join trade unions. U.S. labor law reform has been debated for years, but the debate has focused on specific proposals.

Lance Compa (Cornell School of Industrial and Labor Relations) provides a general overview of recommended changes in U.S. labor law: 1) interim reinstatement of workers fired for union activity and tougher remedies and sanctions to deter violations; 2) closer National Labor Relations Board scrutiny of anti-union statements by employers, with strong and swift remedies for violations; 3) changes to encompass the rights and interests of contingent workers, contract workers, and others in new occupations; 4) stronger remedies for surface bargaining (willful refusal to bargain in good faith); 5) protection of all workers by bringing agricultural workers, domestic workers, and low-level supervisors under National Labor Relations Act coverage; 6) more protection for immigrant workers; and 7) prohibition of permanently replacing workers who exercise the right to strike.

Other essays focus on closing the gap between U.S. labor law and international labor law (which is "very much a part of international human rights law"), occupational health and safety as a core worker right, an assessment of International Labor Organization conventions from an employers' perspective, a defense of current U.S. labor law, why the right to refrain from collective bargaining is no right at all, transnational labor solidarity, and faith community support for workers' organizing.

[NOTE: Labor law reform is unlikely in the present business-friendly Congress, but, some day, perhaps, this is what the future may be like.]

## GOVERNMENT/DEMOCRACY (November 2003)

*The Future of Freedom: Illiberal Democracy at Home and*

*Abroad*. Fareed Zakaria (editor, *Newsweek International*). New York: W.W. Norton, April 2003, 286 p.

We live in a democratic age. Over the last century, the world has been shaped by one trend above all others—the rise of democracy. In 1900, not a single country had what we would today call a democracy: a government created by elections in which every adult citizen could vote (today, 119 do). What is truly distinctive about today's capitalism is not that it is global or technology-driven, but that it is democratic, with consumption, saving, and investment turned into a mass phenomenon, and economic power shifting downward. Culture has also been democratized, and quantity has become quality.

The Internet has taken this process another huge step forward: "the democratization of technology and information means that most anyone can get his hands on anything." And thus the democratization of violence has become one of the most fundamental features of today's world, overriding the state monopoly over the use of force. Like any broad transformation, democracy has its dark sides, yet we rarely speak about them. But what if democracy produces an Islamic theocracy or something like it?

Across the globe, democratically elected regimes are routinely ignoring constitutional limits on their power and depriving citizens of basic rights—the phenomenon of "illiberal democracy" (after all, Adolf Hitler became chancellor of Germany via free elections). Over the last half-century in the West, democracy and liberty have merged. But today *the two strands of liberal democracy are coming apart: "democracy is flourishing; liberty is not."*

Zakaria considers: 1) how the American system is undemocratic (the U.S. Senate is the most unrepresentative upper house in the world, the rich fabric of civil society is wearing thin, political parties are Potemkin organizations, perpetual campaigning and pandering have discredited the system); 2) the history of human liberty (the rise of the Christian church is the most important source of liberty in the West, and liberty led to democracy); 3) the East Asian model (this region is still rife with corruption, nepotism, and voter fraud—but so were most Western democracies, even fifty years ago); 4) the next wave for democracy to flourish and deepen (the most promising major country that has moved toward democracy recently is Mexico; other likely prospects are Belarus, Bulgaria, Croatia, Malaysia, Morocco, Romania, Tunisia, and Turkey); 5) prospects for democracy in China; 6) illiberal democracy in Russia (slipping toward an elected autocracy) and elsewhere; 7) tyranny of the majority in India (a genuinely free and freewheeling society that has become more democratic, but less tolerant, secular, law-abiding, and liberal); (8) the Islamic exception ("Arab rulers of the Middle East are autocratic, corrupt, and heavy-handed; but they are still more liberal, tolerant, and pluralistic than what would likely replace them. On virtually every political issue, the monarchs are more liberal than the societies over which they reign"); 9) the "simple-minded populism increasingly embraced in the U.S." (undermining traditional authority and allowing the triumph of organized interest groups); 10) California's public sector as "an unmitigated mess" (largely because of the extreme form of open, non-party-based, initiative-friendly democracy); 11) the death of authority (the old elites were based on bloodlines but were socially responsible because they were secure in their status; the new system of selecting elites is more democratic, but their interests are narrow and their horizon is "not long term but tomorrow").

In sum, "the twentieth century was marked by two broad trends: the regulation of capitalism and the deregulation of democracy; both experiments overreached." The regulation of capitalism resulted in heavy tax rates and byzantine government controls; the deregulation of democracy produced an unwieldy system unable to govern or command the respect of people.

"Governments will have to make hard choices, resist the temptation to pander, and enact policies for the long term. The only possible way that this can be achieved is by insulating some decision-makers from the intense pressures of interest groups, lobbies, and political campaigns."

This has already happened with the rise of independent central banks like the U.S. Federal Reserve, which has smoothed out the business cycle. The European Union has been effective because it is insulated from political pressures. "What we need in politics today is not more democracy but less" (e.g., the proposal by Alan Blinder for an independent federal tax authority). "If current trends continue, democracy will undoubtedly face a crisis of legitimacy," becoming a system "ruled by organized or rich or fanatical minorities, protecting themselves for the present and sacrificing the future."

> [NOTE: A long view that is very wide-ranging, very well-written, and very astute. Zakaria, who was raised in India and frequently writes for *Newsweek*, may well be the Walter Lippman for our global age.]

## WORLD/U.S. POWER (January 2004) *26:1/010

*America as Empire: Global Leader or Rogue Power?* Jim Garrison (president, State of the World Forum, San Francisco). Foreword by John Naisbitt. San Francisco, Calif.: Berrett-Koehler, February 2004, 224 p.

America has made the transition from republic to empire. It was founded to be a beacon of light unto the nations, a democratic and egalitarian haven. It used to present freedom. Now it represents power. People used to think of the United States as a global leader. Now a majority of the world thinks of it as a rogue power. Although America remains a republic inside its own borders, it has become an empire in relationship with the rest of the world, and there is no turning back.

The central question is what America should do with the power it has. Internally, the transition from republic to empire is almost always made at the cost of freedom, which is lost far more easily than it is gained. Externally, empires incite insurrection; empires have many enemies and few friends. "To achieve greatness, an empire needs a transcendental vision that can unite all its disparate elements within an overarching purpose." It must be a mission that the entire empire can join together to achieve—one that is fundamentally constructive, not destructive.

This book seeks "to challenge Americans at their point of empire to articulate a vision for the world that is worthy of the power they now wield over the world." No one but the United States is even remotely capable of leading this effort to revitalize the international order and develop innovative solutions to global problems. Will the United States allow the magnitude of its power to eclipse the light by which it was founded? Will it seek mastery to dominate or mastery to serve?

If it uses its power to build democracy at the global level, the United States could leave a powerful legacy. To do this, "America must consciously view itself as a transitional empire, one whose destiny at this moment is to act as midwife to a democratically governed global system. Its great challenge is not to dominate but to catalyze."

The Bush administration, so deeply influenced by neo-conservative and evangelical Christian worldviews, obsesses over fighting fire with fire, while ignoring the buckets of water that could put out the flames. It is consumed by a Jacksonian impulse for war and vengeance. "The single most important step the American people must take to provide creative leadership in the world is to stop using 9/11 as an excuse for further retributive action." It is time for constructive politics and healing.

In the spirit of Wilson, Roosevelt, and Truman, the United States should now provide global leadership through the three pillars of its greatness: military strength, economic power, and democratic idealism. 1) Global Security for the International Community: the vast U.S. military forces around the world will have to become as much peacekeepers as warriors, and as much nation builders as destroyers of rogue states; a new International Reconstruction Fund should be specifically dedicated to nation-building; 2) Regulating Private Gain in the Context of the Global Common Good: the World Trade Organization must be reformed, and the process of building compensatory institutions at a global level begun in earnest (e.g., the International Labor Organization should be given peer status with international financial institutions); "the essential challenge is to create a series of checks and balances at the global level"; 3) Supporting Network Democracy and Global Issue Networks: Democracy must be redefined at the global level to pioneer the meaning of network governance, the gateway to effectively managing the global system. "World government is not the solution nor is it politically possible under current conditions."

[NOTE: For more on global issue networks, see *High Noon* by J.F. Rischard (Basic Books, 2002; FS *24:9/410). "The U.S. and the world community must ensure that the next global governance regime is implemented pro-actively, before the catastrophe that will inevitably ensue if our global challenges are not solved. What is at stake is nothing less than the foundations of the first planetary civilization."]

## WORLD/U.S. POWER (January 2004)

*The Imperial Tense: Prospects and Problems of American Empire.* Edited by Andrew J. Bacevich (professor of international relations, Boston University). Chicago, Ill.: Ivan R. Dee, Publisher, September 2003, 271 p.

The author of *American Empire: The Realities and Consequences of U.S. Diplomacy* (Harvard University Press, 2002; FS 25:5/214) assembles the "best writing" on the topic, all but one of the twenty essays written after September 11.

Four camps are identified: 1) the establishment line, dismissing the idea of empire as un-American and rejecting the claim that the United States has become or could ever become an imperial power; 2) the anti-imperialism (Marxist) view, affirming the existence of an American empire and denouncing it as evil; 3) those who acknowledge the reality of empire (often substituting euphemisms like uni-polarity or benign hegemony), and enthusiastically endorse that reality as good for the United States and everyone else; and 4) those who acknowledge empire but do not share the enthusiasm, and see the empire as ending in tragedy.

[NOTE: A fifth position, exemplified by Soros and Garrison (26:1/009/010) acknowledges the United States as empire and urges it to pursue a positive vision for the world.]

1) Back to an Imperial Future? George W. Bush on America's responsibility to lead a mission "to bring the hope of democracy, development, free markets, and free trade to every corner of the world" (introduction to the September 2002 National Security Strategy of the United States), David Rieff on liberal imperialism, Deepak Lal on the need for a Pax Americana, Charles Krauthammer on the unipolar era and the need to act unilaterally, socialist David North on America's drive for world domination; 2) The Nature of American Empire: Peter Bender on the New Rome, Andrew Bacevitch on the challenges of sustaining Pax Americana (no one is really in charge, and popular support is highly contingent), David Marquand of Oxford University on the United States as playground bully (but "simplistic anti-Americanism is equally dangerous"), journalist Martin Walker on the United States as an empire unlike any other, Victor Davis Hanson of the Hoover Institution rejecting the notion of an American empire; 3) Imperial Strategies: Stanley Hoffman on the United States as sheriff and missionary, G. John Ikenberry on imperial ambitions and dangers, Stephen Peter Rosen on imperial choices; 4) Imperial Prospects: Wendell Berry on the potential "radical revision" of U.S. political character, Gabriel Ash on the empire's coming crisis (the new focus on war interferes with business and undermines the credibility of the institutions representing capitalism; "no matter what ensues, the bad blood between the U.S. and the world can be expected to hurt American business interests.")

## WORLD/HUMAN RIGHTS (January 2004)

*The Human Right to Peace.* Douglas Roche (Senate of Canada; chairman, Middle Powers Initiative, Canadian Pugwash, and UN Disarmament Committee). Toronto: Novalis, October 2003, 271 p.

In the twentieth century, at least 110 million people were killed in 250 wars. This is six times the number of war-related deaths as in the nineteenth century. More than 6 million people have died in war since the end of the Cold War, when security should have been improved.

The twenty-first century does not offer many prospects for improvement; in 2001 alone, 37 armed conflicts were fought in 30 countries, and more than 600 million small arms are in circulation around the world.

Some hold that war is a reality and that those who want to end it are mere idealists. But we are not predestined to violence; rather, war comes out of our culture—the way we are socialized to interact with one another. "The central idea of this book is that the culture of war can and must be changed into a culture of peace." Those who engage in peace work are the true realists of our time, while today's idealists are those who think the war culture can be sustained without a worldwide calamity.

Morality and pragmatism have intersected: what we have long known we *should* do, we now know we *must* do to ensure our survival. "Humanity has no other option."

Topics discussed: the cultural roots of violence, effects of the violence in Afghanistan and Iraq, why "a just war" theory is outmoded (we now have machinery to keep the peace, and too many victims of modern wars are innocent civilians), the critical relationship between disarmament and development, the military impact on the environment (pollution of land and water, military land use), the massive lie that nuclear weapons bring security, the potential "terrorist catastrophe" if weapons of mass destruction are used in this new era of suicidal terrorism, the idea of "a culture of peace" (first used at a 1989 conference, and promulgated by UNESCO's Federico Mayor in the 1990s), peace as a "sacred right" (work toward the "right to peace" grew into a major diplomatic effort in the 1990s), the United Nations Program of Action on a Culture of Peace (adopted by the UN General Assembly in 1999), religion as a prime conveyor of the new culture (illustrating essential messages of peace in Islam and all religions, and the fundamentalist opposition in all religions), the 1993 Declaration of a Global Ethic, peace education as a necessary investment in future generations, new nongovernmental organization/civil society demands for a humane world, the growth of the World Social Forum (from 20,000 participants at the first gathering in Porto Alegre in 2001, to 50,000 in 2002, and more than 100,000 from 126 countries in 2003).

An appendix presents the 1997 Declaration by Federico Mayor on "The Human Right to Peace."

[NOTE: A wise and important book that updates the compelling argument for encouraging a culture of peace.]

# Annotated Bibliography (D–I)*

*Only a few of the many books dealing with the future can be listed here. Selection criteria include recency of publication, trustworthiness of the author, readability, and usefulness to nonspecialists. Certain classic works have also been included, as well as a few other books not fully meeting the selection criteria but still likely to be of interest to readers. Information on the most recent books is available on the World Future Society's Web site (wfs.org), which also provides information through* Future Survey—*the best available guide to current literature dealing with the future.*

* Part 2 of four parts, one in each volume in this series. Reprinted with permission from Edward Cornish and the World Future Society.

Dash, Leon. *Rosa Lee: A Mother and Her Family in Urban America.* New York: Basic Books, 1996.

A *Washington Post* reporter tells the story of a mother living on welfare and petty crime in the slums of Washington, D.C. Six of her eight children followed her into welfare and crime, but two chose to make a different life for themselves—and did so. This Pulitzer Prize-winning investigation showed how people in appalling circumstances could choose a better future for themselves.

Dator, James A., ed. *Advancing Futures: Futures Studies in Higher Education.* Westport, Conn.: Praeger, 2002.

A collection of twenty-eight essays bearing on futures studies, with an introduction by the editor, a longtime professor of political science at the University of Hawaii. The contributors are almost exclusively professors who have been active in futures studies. The well-informed papers will mainly interest those teaching futures studies or interested in doing so.

Davidson, Frank P., with John Stuart Cox. *Macro: A Clear Vision of How Science and Technology Will Shape Our Future.* New York: William Morrow, 1983.

Though now dated, this book remains an excellent introduction to macro-engineering—large-scale engineering projects. The author, long active in the American Society for Macro-Engineering, served as the first president of the Institute for the Future, now in Menlo Park, California.

de Jouvenel, Bertrand. *The Art of Conjecture.* Monaco: Editions du Rocher, 1964; Rev. New York: Basic Books, 1967.

This classic of futurist literature discusses basic concepts of thinking about the future. De Jouvenel rejects the notion that there can be a "science of the future," and calls for the study of ideas about what may happen in the future as a means of deciding what actions to take in the present.

Denning, Peter J., ed. *The Invisible Future: The Seamless Integration of Technology into Everyday Life.* New York: McGraw-Hill, 2002.

Eighteen chapters by such authors as Ray Kurzweil, Alan Kay, David Baltimore, and Michael Dertouzos on virtual reality, "ambient intelligence," and other technologies changing our lives in different ways.

Dewar, James A. *Assumption-Based Planning: A Tool for Reducing Avoidable Surprises.* Cambridge, U.K., 2002.

Strategic planner James A. Dewar directs RAND's Frederick S. Pardee Center for Longer Range Global Policy and the Future Human Condition. In his book, he emphasizes the importance of identifying key assumptions in planning and hedging to prevent trouble if these assumptions prove vulnerable. Readable and authoritative, the book should be especially useful to practicing planners.

Diamond, Jared. *Guns, Germs, and Steel: The Fates of Human Societies.* New York: W.W. Norton, 1997.

Diamond argues that environmental factors are primarily responsible for history's broadest patterns, helping to explain such things as the development of agriculture in the Middle East, European colonization of the Americas, and the enormous diversity and primitiveness of cultures in New Guinea. In the context of this fascinating explanation for the technological and material success and/or failure of certain cultures, Diamond argues strongly that history can be a science, though he concedes that certain human personalities do play a significant role in shaping events.

Diderot, Denis. *Encyclopédie, ou Dictionnaire Raisonné des Sciences, des Arts, et des Métiers.* Paris, 1763. Selections edited with notes and introduction by Charles Coulston Gillispie. *A Diderot Pictorial Encyclopedia of Trades and Industry.* 2 vols. New York: Dover Publications, 1959.

The engravings in these volumes provide a fascinating look at what manufacturing was like before the Industrial Revolution.

Didsbury, Howard F., Jr., ed. *Frontiers of the 21st Century: Prelude to the New Millennium.* Bethesda, Md.: World Future Society, 1999.

This collection of twenty papers presented to the 1999 General Assembly deals with topics like the future of God, information technology, genetic engineering, utopias, and the next thousand years.

———. *21st Century Opportunities and Challenges: An Age of Destruction or an Age of Transformation.* Bethesda, Md.: World Future Society, 2003.

Prepared for the society's 2003 conference, this volume provides an excellent introduction to current thinking among leading futurists. The thirty authors (twenty-six papers) include Wendell Bell, Lynn Elen Burton, Vary T. Coates, Amitai Etzioni, Theodore J. Gordon, Jerome C. Glenn, Hazel Henderson, J. Ostrom Moller, Arthur B. Shostak, Richard A. Slaughter, David P. Snyder, Allen Tough, and Ian Wilson.

Diebold, John. *Technology and Social Policy: Meeting Society's 21st Century Needs*. Quincy, Mass.: Management Science Publishing Co., 1997.

A visionary leader in the use of technology to meet human social needs, the author here addresses such issues as getting innovation into politics, finances, railroads, organizations, and more. In 1952, Diebold published a book entitled *Automation* and thus popularized the word he invented for what was happening in leading-edge industries.

Dyson, Freeman. *Imagined Worlds*. Cambridge, Mass.: Harvard University Press, 1997.

A physicist-astronomer offers a wide-angle view of science and science-fiction speculation. He envisions humans spreading out over the universe, taking on different forms as they adapt genetically to different environments.

Easterbrook, Gregg. *The Progress Paradox: How Life Gets Better While People Feel Worse*. New York: Random House, 2003.

Life has improved in the past century, even in the developing world: more food, more money, better health care, etc. Yet many people feel life is getting worse, and the author asks why that should be. One problem is that prosperity does not necessarily bring happiness. But there's much more to be said, and the book makes an interesting and thought-provoking read.

Ellul, Jacques. *The Technological Bluff*. Grand Rapids, Mich.: William B. Eerdmans Publishing Co., 1990.

A French Calvinist continues his long war against modern technological society. Ellul became famous for his 1954 book *La Technique*, translated into English as *The Technological Society*.

Ferkiss, Victor. *Nature, Technology, and Society: Cultural Roots of the Current Environmental Crisis*. New York: New York University Press, 1993.

A wide-ranging, historical study by a noted political scientist of people's attitudes toward nature and technology. Concisely written and highly informative, the volume serves as an excellent historical briefing for understanding the environmental issues that now face us.

Flechtheim, Ossip K. *History and Futurology*. Meisenheim am Glan, Germany: Verlag Anton Hain, 1966.

This collection of essays by a professor of political science who taught in the United States and Germany is now mainly of historical interest. Ossip Flechtheim published a prophetic article entitled "Teaching the Future" in a relatively obscure U.S. publication in 1943. In this article he called for the development of courses dealing with the future. Later he published other articles on what he called "futurology." This volume of essays, written primarily between 1941 and 1952, is about equally divided between history and futurology. During the late 1960s, the author founded the German journal *Futurum*, a scholarly journal devoted to studies of the future.

Fogg, C. Davis. *Team-Based Strategic Planning: A Complete Guide to Structuring, Facilitating, and Implementing the Process*. New York: AMACOM, 1994.

How to structure strategic planning, facilitate the process, and use teamwork smoothly and productively. Includes actual procedural steps, plans for facilitators, and extensive lists of *do*s and *don't*s.

Forrester, Jay W. *World Dynamics*. Cambridge, Mass.: Wright-Allen Press, 1971.

Jay Forrester, long-time professor of management at the Massachusetts Institute of Technology, developed a technique known as "system dynamics" to simulate the functioning of factories, cities, and the world as a whole. The simulation of world trends indicated that catastrophe looms if man does not drastically slow down the growth of population and industrialization. Forrester's colleague, Dennis Meadows, used system dynamics in the *Limits to Growth* study that was widely discussed in the early 1970s.

Fowles, Jib, ed. *Handbook of Futures Research*. Westport, Conn.: Greenwood Press, 1978.

This collection of writings by forty-six futurists, including Arthur C. Clarke, Herman Kahn, Victor Ferkiss, and Theodore Gordon, is a treasure house of ideas about the future. Though now dated, this scholarly book has been skillfully edited and can be used with profit by almost anyone interested in the future.

Fukuyama, Francis. *Our Posthuman Future: Consequences of the Biotechnology Revolution*. New York: Farrar, Straus and Giroux, 2002.

The author worries that if we don't stop tinkering with human biology we may enter a "posthuman" future in which "freedoms" have run amok. What will happen as parents are free to choose the kind of children they have and entrepreneurs are free to pursue the technology for profit? Fukuyama also frets about human embryos, which now have "a moral status somewhere between that of an infant and that of other types of cells and tissues." To what extent are we willing to create and grow embryos for utilitarian purposes?

Gabor, Dennis. *Inventing the Future*. New York: Knopf, 1964.

Dennis Gabor, a Nobel Prize-winning physicist, popularized the phrase "inventing the future." He argues that it is not possible to predict what will happen in the future, but it is possible to create the future through imagination and effort. In this book, Gabor argues that civilization faces three dangers: nuclear war, overpopulation, and "the age of leisure." Gabor suggests that man may be able to cope with the first two dangers more easily than with the third, because of its novelty. In recent decades, man has moved rapidly toward the abolition of work but has done little to prepare himself for leisure. Gabor argues for more creative imagination both in short-range social engineering and in long-term visions of the future.

Galtung, Johan, and Sohail Inayatullah, eds. *Macrohistory and Macrohistorians: Perspectives on Individual, Social, and Civilizational Change*. Westport, Conn.: Praeger, 1997.

A compact and valuable introduction to macrohistory. Separate chapters discuss a score of macrohistorians (Hegel, Marx, Spengler, Toynbee, and others). These big-picture historians do not provide very usable guidance to the future, the editors decided.

Gardner, John W. *Self-Renewal: The Individual and the Innovative Society*. Rev. New York: W.W. Norton, 1981.

In this modern classic, Gardner explains why some individuals and societies atrophy and decay while others remain innovative and creative. Topics discussed include innovation, obstacles, commitment, and meaning; attitudes toward the future; and moral decay and renewal.

Gates, Bill, with Nathan Myhrvold and Peter Rinearson. *The Road Ahead*. New York: Viking, 1995.

After telling how his 1974 vision of the future led to his becoming the world's richest man, Gates gives his new vision of the future: Rapid progress in computers and telecommunications will produce good things for everybody. He admits to a few worries: power failures and the loss of privacy. (He envisions people using videocameras to document every moment of their lives to guard against criminal charges.) This is a readable and informative book by someone whose expertise is heavily credentialed by his wealth.

Gelernter, David. *1939: The Lost World of the Fair*. New York: Free Press, 1995.

"The World of Tomorrow" was the theme of the 1939 New

York World's Fair. Yale professor David Gelernter's vivid account of that fair and its visions of the future includes an assessment of the subsequent success of the fair's expectations of what would happen in the following years.

Georges, Thomas M. *Digital Soul: Intelligent Machines and Human Values*. Boulder, Colo., and Oxford, U.K.: Westview Press, 2003.

An inquiry into the implications of machine intelligence and human values. The author explains how humans can make machines that are smarter than their designers, and analyzes such issues as: How will we distinguish "human" from "machine" in the future? What will happen if machines not only think but have emotions? What if machines become conscious? What rights will they have? A highly readable discussion of the profound questions that advancing machine intelligence is posing for human values.

Gibson, Rowan, ed. Foreword by Alvin and Heidi Toffler. *Rethinking the Future*. Naperville, Ill.: Nicholas Brealey Publishing, 1997.

This collection of essays by such noted business futurists as Charles Handy, John Naisbitt, Lester Thurow, Warren Bennis, Philip Kotler, and Peter Senge offers a cutting-edge look at the new paradigm. Businesses will need to rethink their basic principles as well as changes in competition, control and complexity, leadership, markets, and the world.

Gleick, James. *Chaos: Making a New Science*. New York: Viking 1987.

Though now dated, this may still be the best popular introduction to the science of chaos.

———. *Faster: The Acceleration of Just About Everything.* New York: Pantheon, 1999.

The author of *Chaos* takes a hard look at today's quickreflexed, multi-tasking, channel-flipping, fast-forwarding society.

Glenn, Jerome C., and Theodore J. Gordon. *Futures Research Methodology*. Version 2.0. Paperback, with CD-ROM. Washington, D.C.: American Council for the United Nations University, 2003.

Some twenty-five methods and tools for forecasting and analyzing global change are provided in the latest version of this comprehensive and internationally peer-reviewed handbook. Chapters cover each method's history, primary and secondary uses, strengths and weaknesses, applications, and potential uses. The chapters are presented in both MS Word and PDF formats.

Godet, Michel. *Creating Futures: Scenario Planning as a Strategic Management Tool*. London: Economica, 2001.

A general discussion of scenarios and other future-oriented issues by the head of a future-oriented group at the Paris-based National Conservatory of Arts and Professions.

Halal, William E., ed. *The Infinite Resource: Creating and Leading the Knowledge Enterprise*. San Francisco, Calif.: Jossey-Bass, 1998.

Promising new concepts, lessons, and suggestions for leading the new organizational enterprise are offered by some of the best minds in business and government. Among the contributors are Bell Atlantic CEO Raymond Smith, Indianapolis Mayor Stephen Goldsmith, and networking gurus Jessica Lipnack and Jeffrey Stamps.

Hammond, Debora. *The Science of Synthesis: Exploring the Social Implications of General Systems Theory*. Boulder, Colo.: University Press of Colorado, 2003.

Systems thinking, well documented in this scholarly text, is an important strain in modern scientific thought. Systems thinking emphasizes the relationships and interconnections in biological, ecological, social, psychological, and technical dimensions of human life. These interconnections become extremely important in thinking about the future.

Harper, Stephen C. *The Forward-Focused Organization: Visionary Thinking and Breakthrough Leadership to Create Your Company's Future.* New York: AMACOM, 1999.

Management professor Stephen Harper offers a readable, practical guide to creating a forward-focused organization. He has digested much of the best thinking of the management gurus on strategic management and leading changes, and he neatly sums up many of their most useful insights. He devotes a full chapter to futuring.

Harrison, Lawrence E., and Samuel P. Huntington. *Culture Matters: How Values Shape Human Progress.* New York: Basic Books, 2000.

Two Harvard scholars present an excellent anthology of papers dealing with the influence of culture on economic progress. Thought provoking and readable. Harrison is the author of *Underdevelopment Is a State of Mind.* Huntington is widely known for his best seller, *The Clash of Civilizations and the Remaking of World Order.* Among the causes of underdevelopment are fatalism and negative attitudes toward the future.

Heilbroner, Robert. *Visions of the Future: The Distant Past, Yesterday, Today, Tomorrow.* New York: Oxford University Press and New York Public Library, 1995.

Stretching 50,000 years into the past and "who knows how many into the future," this gracefully written volume explores how humans have viewed the future. Heilbroner argues that there have only been three ways to view the future: The first, which spans from the Stone Age to the 1700s, was that the future would be like the past; the second, spanning from the 1700s to about 1950, is that the future will be better than today; and the third, where we are today, is an ambivalent outlook.

Henderson, Hazel. *Building a Win-Win World: Life Beyond Global Economic Warfare*. San Francisco, Calif.: Berrett-Koehler, 1996.

A provocative economist and futurist examines the havoc that the current economic system is creating globally. Even as new markets emerge worldwide, they are running on old textbook models that ignore social and environmental costs and that will inevitably lead to global economic warfare. Henderson shows how win-win strategies can bring stability and peace to our future.

Herman, Roger E., Thomas G. Olivo, and Joyce L. Gioia. *Impending Crisis: Too Many Jobs, Too Few People*. Winchester, Va.: Oakhill Press, 2002.

The authors foresee a dangerously growing shortage of skilled workers in the years ahead as well as a widening gap in worker skills. The book is designed mainly to provide practical advice for business executives. Herman and Gioia are strategic business futurists concentrating on workforce and workplace trends. Herman is a contributing editor to *The Futurist* magazine. Olivo is a recognized expert in measuring factors that affect bottom-line performance in organizations.

Hesselbein, Frances, Marshall Goldsmith, and Richard Beckhard, eds. *The Organization of the Future*. Drucker Foundation Future Series. San Francisco, Calif.: Jossey-Bass Publishers, 1997.

A collection of forty thoughtful essays on how organizations might reshape themselves for the coming years.

Hicks, David. *Citizenship for the Future: A Practical Classroom Guide*. Godalming, U.K.: WWF-UK, 2001.

A resource book for teachers seeking to teach about environmental issues and the future.

———. *Lessons for the Future: The Missing Dimension in Education*. London: RoutledgeFalmer, 2002.

This book by an outstanding British educator well-experienced in teaching young people about futuring is strongly recommended to educators.

Higgins, James M. *101 Creative Problem Solving Techniques: The Handbook for New Ideas for Business*. Winter Park, Fla.: The New Management Publishing Co., 1994.

Highly readable, useful, and attractively presented descriptions of creative problem-solving methods, such as scenario writing, brainstorming, Delphi polling, use of analogies, role playing, etc.

Hoyle, John R. *Leadership and Futuring: Making Visions Happen*. Thousand Oaks, Calif.: Corwin Press, a division of Sage Publications, 1995.

This short, readable book introduces the use of futuring and visioning mainly to teachers at the high-school level.

Hubbard, Barbara Marx. *Conscious Evolution*. Novato, Calif.: New World Library, 1998.

This highly personalized vision of the human future describes humans evolving toward higher forms of being in which to express their creativity and life purpose. The author, one of the best-known visionaries of spiritual awakening, is founder and president of the Center for Conscious Evolution (San Rafael, California). Her book offers a five-stage plan for human salvation.

Hughes, Barry B. *International Futures: Choices in the Creation of a New World Order*. 2nd ed. Boulder, Colo., and Oxford, U.K.: Westview Press, 1996.

This book and the accompanying software help you to define and develop key concepts in demographics, economics, the environment, and other issues. You can use the software to develop alternative views of our global future.

Huxley, Aldous. *Brave New World*. New York: Harper Row, 1931.

A classic dystopian novel by a writer celebrated for social satires.

Inayatullah, Sohail, and Paul Wildman. *Futures Studies: Methods, Emerging Issues and Civilizational Visions*. CD-ROM. Brisbane, Australia: Prosperity Press, 1999.

What is the long-term future of humanity? Will civilizations violently clash, or are we on the verge of planetary governance? These and other critical questions about the future are addressed in this unique, multimedia CD-ROM. The presentation includes a Reader of methods, emerging issues, and visions; a Gallery of fractal images; a participatory Future Forum, and the Future Coffee Shoppe—an e-mail discussion group and hyper-achieving bulletin board through which you can e-mail authors, converse with other readers, and even initiate a collaboration for future editions. Completing the CD may also help you earn a diploma in futures studies.

# Notes on Contributors

**Tsvi Bisk** is an independent Israeli futurist and strategy analyst. His book, *Futurizing the Jews* (coauthored with Dr. Moshe Dror), has been published by Praeger/Greenwood Press. Tsvi can be reached at bisk@zivgroup.co.il.

**Linda Brown**, formerly a director of senior social services, a science educator, a workforce developer, and an academic adviser, has a special interest in improving the world for all generations. Since earning a master's degree in Studies of the Future at the University of Houston-Clear Lake, she has been reporting to corporate clients on the outlook for American families.

**Ann Coombs** is a thought leader, futurist, and president of Coombs Consulting, Ltd. She speaks internationally on innovative thinking, creativity, and being a "rule breaker" in the corporate world. Ann is the author of the best-seller *The Living Workplace: Soul, Spirit and Success in the 21$^{st}$ Century* (Harper Collins, 2001). Her newsletter on *living* workplaces can be found at www.thelivingworkplace.com. It provides current trends and research on the global workplace, and is read by 250,000 readers worldwide.

**Marilyn Dudley-Rowley**, Ph.D., teaches sociology, political science, and criminal justice courses at Sonoma State University near San Francisco, California. A wide sampling of prior occupations gives her multiple perspectives on the human condition. After a tour-of-duty in the U.S. Army, she hosted and produced radio news shows, did investigations for a number of federal task forces, performed research that helped tailor public lands legislation, worked as an archaeologist and a geoscientist, drove as a long-haul trucker cross-country, worked as a clinical counselor and marriage and family therapist, and participated in a space station simulation in Russia. She is affiliated with NASA, the Department of Defense's Human

Factors Engineering Technical Advisory Group, the World Affairs Council of Northern California, the American Institute of Aeronautics and Astronautics, and other organizations. E-mail: md-r@ops-alaska.com; Web site: www.ops-alaska.com.

**Medard Gabel** has written six books on global issues. His most recent are *Seven Billion Billionaires* and *Global Inc.: An Atlas of the Multinational Corporation*. He worked with Buckminster Fuller for twelve years, and has conducted workshops and consulted for more than four hundred corporations, universities, high schools, and organizations throughout the world, including the United Nations, UNEP, World Bank, General Motors, IBM, Motorola, DuPont, and the governments of the Netherlands, Tanzania, and the United States. More about his work can be found at www.bigpicturesmallworld.com and at www.bigpictureconsulting.com. He can be reached at medard@bigpicturesmallworld.com.

**Thomas Gangale** is an aerospace engineer and a former officer in the U.S. Air Force. He is the executive director of OPS-Alaska, a think tank based in Petaluma, California, and a graduate student in international relations at San Francisco State University. He is the author of the California Plan to reform the presidential nomination process. His writings are available on the OPS-Alaska Web site at www.ops-alaska.com.

**Dr. Sohail Inayatullah** is a professor at Tamkang University in Taiwan and University of the Sunshine Coast in Australia. He is the editor of the *Journal of Futures Studies* and associate editor of New Renaissance (www.ru.org). Books written and edited by Inayatullah include *Macrohistory and Macrohistorians; Understanding Sarkar;* and *Questioning the Future.* He regularly body surfs, meditates, and plays basketball. His Web site: www.metafuture.org.

**Roger Kaufman**, Ph.D., is professor emeritus at Florida State University and director of Roger Kaufman & Associates. His

Ph.D. is in communications from New York University, and he has consulted with public and private organizations in the United States, Canada, Australia, New Zealand, Latin America, and Europe. Kaufman has published 35 books—including *Strategic Thinking* as well as *Mega Planning*—and more than 230 articles on strategic planning, performance improvement, quality management and continuous improvement, needs assessment, management, and evaluation. His e-mail is rkaufman@nettally.com and his Web site is www.megaplanning.com.

**Usha Menon**, Ph.D., is an associate professor of anthropology in the Department of Culture and Communication at Drexel University. She received her Ph.D. from the University of Chicago in 1995. She has written extensively on various aspects of Hindu society and civilization and on Hindu-Muslim relations in contemporary India. Her most recent articles include: "Dominating Kali: Hindu Family Values and Tantric Power" (coauthored with R.A. Shweder) in Rachel McDermott and Jeffrey Kripal (eds.), *Encountering Kali: In the Margins, at the Center, in the West*, (Berkeley, Calif.: University of California Press, 2003); "Exploring the 'Militancy' of Hindu Women," *Nationalism and Ethnic Politics* (2003: 2); and, "Multicultural Feminism: Deepening Parochial Feminist Sensibilities" submitted for publication to *Signs*.

**Robert J. Merikangas**, Ph.D., is an independent scholar, a retired librarian, and an adjunct professor at the University of Maryland-College Park. His current writing interests focus on a matrix of resources for faithful citizens. Citizens are part of the "wisdom community." See "Heuristics for Wisdom Communities," *Futures Research Quarterly*, 14:2 (Summer 1998).

**Malcolm Morgan** is a creative writer and journalist. His focus is on human rights, social justice, and family and youth issues.

**Jim Pinto** was the founder and former CEO of a high-technology company in San Diego, California. He is now a technology futurist, angel investor, speaker, writer, commentator, and consultant. His recent book, *Automation Unplugged*, was published by ISA. He invites your feedback, ideas, suggestions, and encouragement. Visit his Web site: JimPinto.com; or e-mail: jim@jimpinto.com.

**David Reynolds**, Ph.D., trains the next generation of union leaders through the many programs offered by the Labor Studies Center at Wayne State University. His recent publications include: *Partnering for Change: Unions and Community Groups Build Coalitions for Economic Justice* and *Taking the High Road: Communities Organize for Economic Change* (both from M.E. Sharpe, Armonk, N.Y.). He continues to organize living wage coalitions in Michigan and is facilitating a national research project documenting how unions and their allies are building regional political and economic power. Reynolds received his Ph.D. from Cornell University. E-mail: aa2589@wayne.edu.

**Patrick G. Salsbury** is a design scientist living in the San Francisco Bay Area. He works on creating solutions for social problems, such as traffic congestion, homelessness, poverty, hunger, water shortage, and poor education. He is the founder of Reality Sculptors: http://reality.sculptors.com/.

**Chris Seiple** is the president of the Institute for Global Engagement, an international religious freedom "think tank with legs."

**Arthur B. Shostak**, Ph.D. (Editor), holds the title of Emeritus Professor of Sociology after recently retiring from Drexel University (Philadelphia, Pennsylvania), where he had been a professor since 1967. Since he began college teaching in 1961, he has specialized in trying to apply sociology to real-time problems ("challenges") and in shaping and communicating long-range forecasts. While at Drexel, he directed a two-year study of teenage attitudes toward the world of work and related matters. He has written, edited, and coedited more than thirty books and more than 160 articles, and was presented with the Pennsylvania Sociological Society's Distinguished Sociologist Award in 2004. He especially recommends his 2003 edited collection, *Viable Utopian Ideas: Shaping a Better World* (M.E. Sharpe, Armonk, N.Y.). You can contact him at shostaka@drexel.edu.

# Index

303.49          $28.00
Tac
Tackling tomorrow today. Volume
two, America moving ahead

| | | DATE DUE | |
|---|---|---|---|
| | | | |
| | | | |
| | | | |
| | | | |
| | | | |
| | | | |
| | | | |
| | | | |
| | | | |
| | | | |
| | | | |